Geoffrey Grogan ~~~~~~~~~~~~ g and writing the best ~~~~~~~~~~~~~~~~ New Testament as well as decades of experience training students for Christian service in almost every imaginable context. Clarity of thought, a gentle and irenic spirit, sanity of judgment and an obvious love for Christ mark all his work. *Wrestling With The Big Issues* well illustrates these much-needed qualities. It combines careful exposition of the mind of Paul with practical application in tune with the apostle's heart. Not only individuals, but also Bible study groups and entire Christian fellowships could benefit enormously by an ongoing study of these pages and a willingness to put their lessons into practice.

Sinclair B Ferguson

This book about Paul is remarkable for being written by a New Testament scholar in such a simple and relevant way that any reader will be able to understand what is being said and see how Paul's letters still speak to Christians today. In a series of topically arranged chapters the author develops Paul's understanding of the Christian life for individuals and the church and calls us back to the apostolic model and teaching. This is a book which could form an excellent basis for discussion in a house group or similar gathering.

I Howard Marshall

*Wrestling with
the
Big Issues*

Geoffrey W. Grogan

Christian Focus Publications

© 1993 Geoffrey W Grogan
ISBN 1 85792 051 1

Published by
Christian Focus Publications Ltd
Geanies House, Fearn, Ross-shire,
IV20 1TW, Scotland, Great Britain.

Scripture quotations are from the New International
Version, published by Hodder & Stoughton

Printed and bound in Great Britain by
Cox & Wyman Ltd, Reading, Berkshire.

Cover design
by
Donna Macleod

Contents

To *Eva*
Encourager, Loving Critic, Wife

Foreword

It has often been suggested that if the Apostle Paul was interviewed as a candidate for a leadership position in a local church today - he might well fail to get the job! A dogmatic, anti-feminist, jailbird of unprepossessing appearance, with a dubious past, would scarcely have much of a chance!

For too long we have maintained a stained-glass impression of the great apostle. We have created a remote image of superhuman godliness which is way beyond our understanding or imitation. Meanwhile, first century Roman civilisation is expanded to reflect the cultural understanding of the UK in the twentieth century.

Clearly these errors need redressing. Paul should be viewed as he was, against his own backdrop, and yet voicing truths which remain unchanged today. In this remarkable endeavour Geoffrey Grogan is astonishingly successful.

I believe that evangelicals must continually return to their Biblical roots for instruction and example. Our understanding and experience need to be sharpened by a deeper acquaintance with God's word through his Spirit - and most of us require help in this department.

Geoff Grogan and I first met when he was one of my tutors at theological college in the 1960s. Known as the 'gentle giant' he possessed the uncanny knack of translating what might appear to be dull doctrine into exciting reality. He knew what it was to set truth on fire. In this book I believe he has achieved exactly that! The personality of the apostle shines through its pages - the life and times of a man who Christ used to transform the history of his Church.

I suspect that this book has an underlying subversive purpose. If our churches today would struggle to accept Paul then it is we who need to change. Furthermore, we need modern-day counterparts with transformed lives like that of Saul of Tarsus which can be transformed into spiritual usefulness.

Clive Calver
General Director, Evangelical Alliance
30 July 1993

1

Introduction

'*Almost certainly the most hated man in Christian history.*'
Who is this?
Paul!

If you love Paul's epistles and have a deep respect for the man himself you may be astounded to learn that these words refer to him.

Be in no doubt about it, though, there is truth in them. Why? For several reasons.

Many of his Jewish contemporaries hated him. Sure enough, when he preached the good news of Jesus in their synagogues, there were usually some who responded positively. Often though there were far more who scornfully rejected the message he brought (Acts 13:45; 17:13, etc.). In fact, Luke tells us, a group of them once banded together and said they would eat nothing until they had killed him (Acts 23:12-15).

It is more surprising to find people who profess allegiance to Jesus and yet have a hearty dislike of Paul's teaching. At the close of the last century and the beginning of this, quite a number of books were written with titles like, '*Jesus or Paul?*' The question implies that a choice has to made between them. Of course, put like that, the reader feels himself compelled to reply, 'Jesus, of course!'

Why pose such a choice ? Because, so it was said, Jesus taught a very simple gospel about the fatherhood of God, the brotherhood of men and the infinite value of every human soul, while Paul changed Christianity into something radically different. Instead of calling people simply to accept the teaching of Jesus he devised a theology of salvation by blood atonement.

The German theologian, Rudolf Bultmann, understood Paul's theology very well, as a passage in one of his books makes very clear. Summarizing Paul's thought about the meaning of the cross, he says, 'The Jesus who was crucified was the pre-existent, incarnate Son of God, and as such He was without sin. He is the Victim whose blood atones for our sins. He bears vicariously the sin of the world, and by enduring the punishment for sin on our behalf He delivers us from death.' [2]

This summary certainly does justice to Paul's teaching in a way almost worthy of John Calvin, John Owen or John Murray. Bultmann makes no attempt here, as some earlier liberal writers did, to try to make Paul say something different from what he appears to be saying. So far, so good.

Read on though. What does Bultmann say in comment on this summary? 'This mythological interpretation is a hotchpotch of sacrificial and juridical analogies which have ceased to be tenable today.'[3] Seeing so clearly what Paul was driving at, he totally rejects it, and this is true of more than Bultmann.

Many modern people dislike Paul's social views, or rather what they think these were. For instance, in passages like Ephesians 5:21-6:9 and Colossians 3:18-4:1, he deals with relationships in the church. In these passages, so it seems, he goes along with slavery and actually fosters male domination of society. If certain modern trends continue, it may well be that his comments on the relation of parents to children will eventually put him out of favour still more.

If this is a true understanding of him (and that is a big 'if'!) then we might conclude that he is not only hopelessly out of date, but that he could easily become the patron saint of the social reactionaries of our era.

The Liberationist and Feminist group of theologians are of course very concerned about social issues of this type. It is not surprising, then, to find that where they have strong influence, Paul is not much in favour.

Mind you, it is true that, for many New Testament scholars, some of these problems are not what they were. For various reasons, Paul's authorship of some of the letters that bear his name is questioned today. The three Pastoral Epistles (1 and 2 Timothy and Titus), Ephesians, Colossians and 2 Thessalonians have all been denied to him by some modern scholars. Even some who do not entirely accept these views have got into the habit, when they document general statements on Paul's life and thought, of using only the seven remaining epistles.

So, it is sometimes pointed out, by those who take this point of view, that Paul does not in fact admonish wives, children and slaves to be subject to their husbands, parents and masters, because it is only in Ephesians and Colossians that he is represented as saying this, and these are among the books of doubtful authorship.

This is not the way we intend to view Paul's writings. There are plenty of good reasons why all thirteen of the letters that claim to be by him may still be treated as authentically Pauline.[4] We will therefore base this work on all thirteen epistles, plus Luke's account in Acts, which also we believe to be an accurate representation of the truth about him.[5]

We will try to take Paul seriously, no matter what he says, despite the problems this may raise for us from time to time. In any case, the views of the scholars who hold a minimizing view on the authorship issues have not always reached the people in the pew, who would perhaps still need help on the difficulties his letters raise for us today.

So, why Paul?

In view of the image of Paul many have today, it might appear strange to be publishing a book on Paul and the way he faced his problems. Won't it be at best an interesting historical survey with no relevance whatever for today's people in today's world?

Not only are our world and Paul's poles apart - that is to be expected - but this would seem to be true also of attitudes. What can this man possibly have to say and, even more important, what can God possibly say through him, that would have the slightest bearing on the modern world or on the church at the end of the 20th Century?

A very great deal. There are in fact many close parallels between his world and ours, and also between the 1st and 20th Century churches. Soon we will be exploring these.

Even so, would it not be better to expect to hear God speak about our problems through somebody more sympathetic to our contemporary concerns?

Luke perhaps. Now there is a man of obviously broad sympathies, sensitive to the needs of the disadvantaged! See how many people like that are mentioned in his Gospel! There are women, children, tax-collectors (rich but hated), Samaritans, beggars and so on - and Jesus touched them all with his grace and blessing.

Alternatively, what about James? Modern seekers after

justice could not wish for anything more apt than the opening of James 5. 'Now listen, you rich people, weep and wail because of the misery that is coming upon you.... Look! The wages you failed to pay the workmen who mowed your fields are crying out against you.' What indignation! Even 8th Century prophets like Amos and Isaiah, for all their profound social concern, rarely come over quite as fiercely as James does in this passage. He hated class snobbery too: see the comments he makes on it in chapter 2 of his letter!

But Paul? Yes, Paul. Please read on.

In actual fact, when we look at what he actually wrote and read it carefully, we get some surprises. This man turns out to have been profoundly sensitive, courteous and tactful. He had a social concern that was both wide and deep. In other words, he was nothing like the caricature many people, even many Christians, seem to have in their minds.

In this study, you see, we will need to expect surprises. We will find Paul, man of his time as he undoubtedly was, to be also a man for our time. Through this man God has many lessons to teach us, not only in theology (we might expect that) but also in the whole field of human relations, both inside and outside the church of Christ.

Most of all, we will discover he did not find living the Christian life easy. Each new day brought its problems and his Divine calling presented him with big issues that were not to be solved overnight. If he were around today, we might find him surprisingly sensitive to many of our own difficulties. It is good then to find we can identify with him to some extent at least.

Many readers of this book may well share with its author a belief in the inspiration and supreme authority of the Bible. They will therefore be used to the idea that Paul's teaching has Divine authority behind it and must be taken seriously.

It is very important, though, to appreciate that this does not mean he was a perfect Christian. Perfect godliness is restricted to one man - the Man, Christ Jesus. Paul had his faults and failings, so that there may be times when, although accepting the authority of his teaching, we will learn from the study of his actual conduct how not to act!

Such times are, however, likely to be comparatively rare. What we can be sure of is that we will learn much that will be of great practical help as we seek to live as Christians in the world of today.

One special advantage in studying Paul is that there is plenty of material available. How varied it is too! We can see him wrestling with theological problems, handling all kinds of church problems from blatant heresy to prickly human beings, facing all kinds of personal sufferings, and, of course, not as a plaster saint but as a sinner saved by grace.

How are we to view him?

The way you view another person will tell me something about you as well as about him or her. A lot will depend on your background, your character and the particular interests and convictions you have. So Keck and Furnish are right when they remind us that there are several Pauls, three at least: the public Paul, the scholar's Paul and the church's Paul. [6]

The history of modern Pauline scholarship, for instance, shows considerable division of opinion. [7]

Albert Schweitzer saw him as an apocalyptic preacher and Christian mystic. So he proclaimed Christ's return to judge the world but also experienced intimate fellowship with God in him.

Rudolf Bultmann was deeply influenced by a particular modern philosophy called existentialism, which lays much emphasis on the importance of creative decision-making, and he reckoned Paul's letters to be classics of Christian existentialism.

For W. D. Davies Paul was a Christian rabbi and all he wrote is to be understood in terms of his Pharisaic background.

Johannes Munck argued that he should be thought of primarily as the apostle of the Gentiles, with an overmastering sense of the importance of the Gentile mission to which God had called him.

Now the interesting thing is that a case has been well made for each of these views of Paul. So there must then be some truth in each of them.

An objective examination of the evidence provided by Acts and his epistles too makes us aware that he was a man of many parts. It is not easy therefore to decide where to begin, or whether he had some integrating role that bound all his diverse interests and functions together.

He was, of course *a writer*. That would be the most obvious fact about him for the man or woman who opens the New Testament for the first time, looking perhaps at the Contents Page.

But how many people decide at an early stage of life to be writers? Very few, except perhaps in poetry and fiction. If you are going to write non-fiction of any real value, you will require much more than a writing gift. Nonsense is no less nonsensical for being expressed in beautiful language! You need knowledge, training and, most of all, for certain types of writing, experience. If we could have asked Paul, a few days after his conversion, what he was going to do for Christ, we would hardly expect him to say, 'I will be a writer.'

He was also *an evangelist and church planter*. If his letters are the major source of our knowledge of him, the Acts of the Apostles (which, incidentally, never mentions them) comes next, and it is his evangelistic and church-planting roles that emerge most clearly there. Through him and his team of fellow-workers many people were won for Christ and many churches were established, particularly in the areas we now know as Turkey and Greece.

But both Acts and the letters show us that his gifts and roles cannot be restricted to writing and church-planting. The letters themselves were penned out of a concern for these churches and this concern went on for many years beyond their founding. Also he did not show this concern only for churches he had planted personally. He evidently saw nothing inappropriate in writing a long letter to the church at Rome. Not only had he had no hand at all in establishing it; he had never even visited it.

The young churches were certainly not without their problems. Quite frequently we find Paul assuming the difficult role of *a trouble-shooter*. He fulfilled this both by visits and by letters.

How did he approach the problems referred to him by churches? He must have had some basic principles in his mind in all his dealings with them.

What kind of principles were they? Ethical? Pastoral? Yes, but they were also deeply theological. In fact his ethical and pastoral convictions cannot be detached from his theology. Rather they are practical implications of it. It was what he believed about God, about Christ, about salvation and about the nature of Christ's church, that determined the counsel he gave local churches.

It is not surprising then that many people think of Paul primarily as *a theologian*, a great Christian thinker. There are many passages in his letters that compel us, as we read, to think deeply about the Christian faith and its meaning. Even so, 'theologian' will not do as a comprehensive definition of his role.

Mark you, he was much closer to the theologian with commitment, the ideal promoted by the Liberation theologians, than to the traditional image of the 'armchair' or 'ivory tower' theologian. Theology for him was never simply a mental exercise. What he believed determined his actions and the whole direction of his life.

We need a category that will embrace all the diverse roles we have considered so far. What is there that includes Paul the writer, Paul the evangelist and church-planter, Paul the trouble-shooter, Paul the theologian? There is just one word, and there can be little doubt that Paul would have approved of our choice of it.

He was *an apostle*. All the tasks he undertook were taken up as an apostle. Whatever he did, he did with authority. He believed this authority was given to him by a special revelation of Christ, and that in that revelation he was called to be and constituted as an apostle. That is why he was so concerned to defend his apostleship against attacks made on it. Destroy his apostolic status and you destroy his life-work.

But, you might object, surely this is not true! Even if he was not recognised as an apostle, he would at least have been a *Christian*. Surely that counts for something!

Yes, indeed it does. Everything of lasting worth Paul ever did after his conversion was the result of that experience and of the relationship with Christ which began then. He became Christ's man, and it was as Christ's man that his

Master appointed him to service as an apostle.

This means then that his standing as a Christian is an even deeper fact about him than his role as an apostle, for the latter was grounded in the former. Should we not then simply declare that his diverse functions find their point of integration in the fact that he was a Christian?

No! True as it is, it is not adequate.

No doubt it would be interesting to study the life and teaching of Erastus, Corinth's city treasurer, or Epaphroditus, the faithful Christian worker, or Phoebe the deaconess, all of whom are mentioned in his letters, although in fact we do not have enough material. If however we are going to get real help with the problems that face us in today's church, we are really in need of something authoritative, and an apostle taught with special authority.

It is sometimes said we should get back to the New Testament church and model ourselves on it. But think what this means! Isn't this a mistake and potentially a very serious one?

Which church? The church at Corinth? What about its party-spirit, its pride in wisdom, its moral standards or lack of them? Are we to copy these? The church at Rome? With its division over practical issues like meat-eating? The church at Thessalonica? What about its lazy members who were content to sleep away time and opportunity until the return of Christ? The church at Philippi, with the tension that existed between Euodia and Syntyche?

Which church? You only have to ask the question seriously and think of the possible answers to know that not even the best of them was good enough to act as a model, although of course we can learn much from any one of them.

We need what the New Testament churches needed, and

what in Paul and the other apostles they had. We need authoritative teaching, the mind of the Lord on the practical issues of church life. In other words, we need to view Paul as an apostle.

We still need though to remember that the whole of Paul's Christian life cannot be subsumed under the apostolic category. We may therefore learn something negatively as well as positively from the way he related to people, as well as gaining much from the authoritative teaching the risen Christ commissioned him to transmit.

Christian and apostle - this is the Paul we will be studying as he faced a whole range of problems. We need to ask God to give us light through him on some of our own. He wrestled with the big issues, as we also must do, and he did so with God.

References

1. L. E. Keck, who wrote these words, goes on to say, 'Probably no other Christian has been hated so intensely as Paul ... Paul is far from everybody's favorite Christian' (*Paul and his letters*. Philadelphia. 2nd Edn. 1988. p.4)

2. R. Bultmann, writing in H. W. Bartsch (ed.). *Kerygma and Myth*, trans. R. H. Fuller. Vol. 1. London. 1953. p.35

3. *ibid*.

4. It is outside the purpose of this book to deal with such questions, but those who wish to follow them up should consult Donald Guthrie. *New Testament Introduction*. 3rd Edn. (revised in 1 vol.) Leicester. 1970 Chapters 15 and 17-19, or D. A. Carson, D. Moo, L. Morris. *An Introduction to the New Testament*. Grand Rapids. 1992

5. Again see D. Guthrie, *op.cit*. chapter 9, or D. A. Carson, D. Moo, L. Morris. *op.cit*. Chapter 6

6. L. E. Keck and V. P. Furnish. *The Pauline Letters*. Nashville. 1984. pp. 11-27

7. For the history of the interpretation of Paul in modern times, see L. E. Keck, *Paul and his Letters*. Philadelphia. 2nd Edn. 1988. pp. 126-158

2

The Background to Paul

Before we can study the actual problems Paul faced, we have some work to do. To feel the force of these problems, we must know something about Paul's own situation.

We need then to look at the world of Paul's own day. We must know something too about the infant and yet swiftly developing Christian movement. Most of all, perhaps, we must know something about his own experience.

You see, you and I belong to the world of the 20th Century and when we read the Bible we are conditioned by that fact. The church of our time bears the marks of its two thousand years of history. Most of all, of course, no two of us are the same, and our individuality determines the way we look at things.

We will need some historical imagination. The pupils of a fine teacher of Roman history said of him, 'He took you by the scruff of the neck and put you into ancient Rome.' That's what a good historical imagination does for you. Of course, it is no good letting your imagination wander freely at will. It must be disciplined all the time by the facts in so far as we can get to grips with them.

What factor or factors most influenced Paul? Scholars are not all agreed on this. Even so, everybody recognises that there were three main elements.

First of all, there was Judaism.

Paul told the Philippians he was a member of the tribe of Benjamin. His Jewish name, Saul, was borne by the most eminent son of this tribe, Israel's first king. It is true, of course, that King Saul came to grief eventually (what a subject he would have been for a Shakespearean tragedy!), but this has not stopped Jews from taking his name. Modern Jews named Saul certainly aren't called after Saul of Tarsus!

Where was he born? Not in Palestine but in Tarsus, the capital of the Roman province of Cilicia. He was therefore a Jew of the Dispersion. This term denotes Jews dispersed in various places in the non-Jewish world.

At one time scholars were inclined to polarize the difference between Palestinian and Dispersion Jews (especially those of the latter who lived in the Mediterranean area) rather too much. There certainly were differences but these can be overstated. In fact most of the Jews of the Mediterranean world were just as keen to keep the Law of Moses as those in Palestine. Distance prevented them, except through pilgrimage on rare occasions, from taking part in the temple worship. If anything, this deprivation tended to endear the Law to them even more and they tried to obey its every dictate.

How were they marked out from their Gentile neighbours? By two things in particular. There was Sabbath-keeping, which affected them weekly, and there were the food laws, which influenced them every single day of their lives.

Sometimes a minority group in a community may not have particularly strong convictions. If this is the case, there may be tendencies to syncretism (combining beliefs or practices of distinct religions) and there may even be absorption by the dominant body.

Where, however, there is great strength of conviction - as there undoubtedly was among the Jews - distinctives are upheld and strict discipline is maintained in the community. This is to ensure that the tradition is passed on from generation to generation. We can see this, for instance, among the Amish people of the eastern United States and among some of the Asian immigrant communities in Britain. It was a feature of Judaism wherever it went, as it still is today particularly among orthodox Jews.

Can we learn anything from this? Surely we can!

Christians should be *well-taught*. We should have convictions, well based in Scripture, and not simply opinions. This is particularly important in the increasingly post-Christian society of Britain and many other western countries today, Of course, we don't need to be paranoiac or extremist in dress or manner of life, but neither should we try to melt indistinguishably into our cultural environment.

In Paul's family home the Sabbath would be kept strictly and the dietary regulations adhered to very carefully. Also his father and mother would teach the moral standards of the Old Testament to the children, and they would put them into practice in the family life.

Inevitably this meant they would be rather isolated socially except from other members of the Jewish community in Tarsus. It would be very difficult, for instance, to accept invitations to meals. Jewish children would usually accept this element of isolation as a normal part of Jewish life, and this would probably have been true of the youthful Paul.

Despite this isolation, many of their Gentile neighbours

would respect the Jews for their austere monotheism and their high moral standards.

In fact, young Paul would often meet 'God-fearers' in the local synagogue. These people had become a regular feature of the Dispersion synagogues. Who were they? Gentiles who had come to a warm appreciation of Judaism, particularly for its ethical monotheism. Instead of going to the pagan temples they would make their way to the synagogues. The challenge was always there to take on board also its less attractive features by the full commitment involved in being a proselyte. They were however welcome to come to the services even if they did not feel they could go as far as this.

Paul labels himself 'a Hebrew of Hebrews' (Phil. 3:5). What precisely did he mean by this term? We cannot be quite sure, although it is almost certain to have had linguistic connotations for him.

He may have meant he was able to read the Hebrew in which the bulk of the Old Testament was written. On the other hand, 'Hebrew' here may be a looser designation of Aramaic, the kindred language which was the *lingua franca* of much of western Asia and the common language of Palestine at this time.

Whatever the exact significance of the phrase, it functions in Philippians 3 as part of a statement of Paul's clear and definite Jewish commitment in his pre-Christian days. Not only in terms of lineage but also of language he was a Jew through and through.

Don't forget though that he was a tent-maker! By pursuing this trade he would get involved in the commercial world of Tarsus. Commerce is in fact the chief justification for and the chief means of spreading a *lingua franca*.

Without a shadow of doubt, this man would have learned Greek as soon as the boundaries of his world began to stretch beyond the walls of his home. To prepare him, his parents may have taught him the language even earlier.

He makes much use of the Septuagint in his letters. This Greek version of the Old Testament had been produced in Alexandria several generations before the coming of Christ. It was the standard Greek translation throughout the synagogues of the Graeco-Roman world. So, whatever Semitic tongues he used, he was also acquainted with the Scriptures in their Greek form.

In terms of his education and party affiliation he was thoroughly Jewish too. To be a Pharisee meant (both outside and inside Palestine) that you were thoroughly committed to the Law.

Pharisaism has had a very bad press among Christians for centuries. In recent years, however, that image has been questioned. This is partly at least in the interests of better relations between Jews and Christians, but it has also been challenged at the scholarly level, largely through the work of E. P. Sanders. Some have blamed the New Testament writers, especially Paul and the author of the Fourth Gospel, for the bad image. This is in fact highly questionable.

Luke records Paul's claim that he was educated in Jerusalem under the tutelage of Gamaliel (Acts 22:3). This probably means he showed considerable promise early on, for Gamaliel was one of the most eminent Rabbis of his day and it would be a great privilege to be one of his students.

Gamaliel was himself a pupil of Hillel, the leader of the less rigorous of two groups of an earlier generation of Rabbis. Rather more than the rival school of Shammai, the school of Hillel was inclined towards applications of the

Law which took into account the changed circumstances
brought about by many centuries of Jewish history.

Does this mean that Paul would have been more open to
the Christian gospel than if he had been reared in the stricter
school? Not necessarily. The debates and differences
between these two schools were never about the nature or
functions or identity of the Messiah, and the Messianic
issue was, without doubt, the central point of division
between Christian and non-Christian Jews.

Remember too that Gamaliel favoured a 'wait and see'
policy as far as the Christian faith was concerned (Acts
5:33-39), but that Paul was bent on persecuting the Christians (Acts 9:1,2). The pupil was therefore much more
anti-Christian than the teacher.

There was also Hellenism

The Greeks were a remarkable people. Not only did they
produce great artists, architects and athletes, but they were
pre-eminent in the world of thought. Not until the 18th
Century Germans did any other people in the western world
produce a major series of great philosophers, and the
Germans, for the most part, addressed questions actually
raised and tackled by the Greeks.

Alexander the Great was the pupil of one of the greatest
of the Greek philosophers, Aristotle. From his father, Philip
of Macedon, Alexander learned the arts of war and not a
little of its cruelty and unscrupulousness, but from Aristotle
he learned respect for fine culture and even some of the
gentler virtues.

Alexander and his army raced, as few others have done
before or since, through great tracts of country. He subdued
lands from the Adriatic to the Indus and from the Crimea to

the Sudan. After his death, his empire was split up into three parts, but common to them all was the Greek culture Aristotle had taught him to admire and which he himself had exported to every land he had conquered.

It did not, of course, replace the native cultures. In each case the two, the more refined incomer and the less refined native, produced some kind of amalgam, differing somewhat of course from place to place as the indigenous cultures changed. We describe this kind of culture as Hellenistic to distinguish it from the Hellenic culture of the Greeks themselves.

Hellenism had come to Cilicia and was well established in Tarsus, its capital. There in fact a great university had been established. This was a little behind Athens and Alexandria in reputation yet it could be referred to in the same breath as those two great centres of learning. Students came to it from all over the known world, and they showed great enthusiasm for learning.

Was Paul himself a student there? We do not know. It is certainly not impossible. In fact, it would be perfectly consistent with the evidence of his letters and also of the Lukan presentation of him in Acts.

He quotes from Greek philosophers at times. As we shall see, the address Luke records him as delivering at the court of the Areopagus in Athens certainly shows he knew what made the Stoics and the Epicureans tick. Some scholars have found the influence of Greek rhetorical forms, especially those of the Cynic and Stoic diatribes, in the argumentative sections of his letters.

Even if there were nothing of this, his style of writing shows the influence of a good education. It is not simply that it is full of quotation and allusion from the Hebrew Scriptures but that it also has a rich Greek vocabulary. He was obviously thoroughly at home in the Greek language. He was able to express his thought tersely and concisely on one occasion, in majestic and sonorous phrases on another. He knew the nuances of words and could employ literary devices like *double entendre* to good effect.

This is not always treated though as evidence for education at Tarsus University. Although the word 'Pharisees' is often thought to mean 'the separated ones', indicating their concern to keep aloof from alien contaminating influences, it is now often argued that isolation from Greek culture was never complete, even among the Pharisees, and even in the Palestinian homeland of the Jews.

So we must enter the verdict of 'not proven' on the theory of a Greek university education as far as Paul is concerned.

What then of the widely disseminated view that his theology was deeply influenced by alien systems of thought coming from Hellenistic culture? For instance, do important themes in his theology show the influence of the mystery-cults that were so strong in parts of the Mediterranean world?

We should not forget that these cults specialized in mysteries, in secrets. As R. A. Cole says, 'We do not know what the mystery was. No uninitiated person did; so it is *a priori* unlikely that Paul the Jew would have known any more than we do.' [1]

What about Gnosticism? Students of early church history are familiar with the major Gnostic cults of the Second Century. Did they exist though in germinal form in Paul's day? Was Gnosticism, as Rudolf Bultmann believed, actually pre-Christian? He maintained it was a generalized phenomenon, emphasising initiation rites and special knowledge, and telling the myth of a Redeemer coming to rescue an intellectual/spiritual elite from its involvement in this material world. Early Christianity, in his view, took over these notions and identified the mythical Redeemer with Jesus[2].

In fact, the existence of pre-Christian Gnosticism cannot be proved. We just do not have clear evidence of the combination of these ideas and especially of the linking at this stage of a redeemer mythology with concepts of secret knowledge[3].

So, while we should recognise the importance of the Greek background to Paul, we must not exaggerate it. Does the Paul who meets us in the epistles really seem to have the outlook or even the temperament of a syncretist? There is in his writings a clear decisiveness as well as a strong dependence on an authoritative Old Testament that makes it seem highly unlikely that he would have - or even that he could have - produced a system of religious thought which was a compound of Judaism and Hellenism.

There was also a Roman element in his background.
He was a Roman citizen and was freeborn. This means that the Romans must have awarded citizenship to his father or to some ancestor who had passed it on to him. This was a great advantage.

Especially it gave him a special standing before the Roman law. When Ludwig van Beethoven was involved in litigation, proceedings were held up for a while. Why? Because in Germany at that time aristocrats, who were designated by the word 'von' before their surnames, had special privileges in law, and the court wanted to find out if

Beethoven's 'van' (from his Dutch extraction) was an equivalent, which, in fact, it was not.

Saul, as Paul (strictly speaking, Paulus) had a Roman name. His citizenship had to be taken seriously by the authorities, and it is interesting to note that he did not hesitate to use this advantage if the cause of Christ could be served in this way (Acts 16: 37; 22:25-29; 25:8-12).

If Paul had not been a Roman citizen, he might never have got to Rome at all, and the latter part of his life would probably have been very different.

Where was he when he wrote his Imprisonment Epistles (Ephesians, Philippians, Colossians and Philemon)? The traditional answer, of course, is Rome, but good arguments have been advanced for some such place as Caesarea or Ephesus. The case against Rome has not been conclusively proved and a Roman location is still accepted by many scholars. The issue is not of great importance in terms of the theme of this book, and so we will assume these letters were penned from Rome [4].

To be in Rome was to be at the centre of the communication network of the ancient world. Probably the Christian 'grapevine' was particularly active there too. It was because his visitors came to him bringing news from the churches that Paul was able to write to them as he did.

There are a number of traces of the Roman world in what he wrote. The Christian's armour of Ephesians 6 was surely based on that of the Roman soldier guarding him at the time! His references to our adoption as sons of God reflect Roman adoption conventions. He told the Philippians they were a colony of heaven, employing a word the Romans used of cities whose citizens enjoyed privileges identical with those of the people of Rome itself.

W. G. de Burgh, in his great work, *The Legacy of the Ancient World*,[5] sought to trace the various elements which, in combination, produced the world of the period of the Renaissance and Reformation, and which, through those two movements, have profoundly shaped modern life. He looked briefly at influences from Egypt, Mesopotamia, and other ancient civilisations, but he concluded that Israel, Greece and Rome have had far, far more creative impact than those emanating from any other source.

Paul inherited all three.

So have we, and so, because of this, the task of understanding him is made that much easier.[6]

References

1. R. A. Cole. 'The Life and Ministry of Paul' in F. E. Gaebelein. *The Expositor's Bible Commentary*. Vol. 1. Grand Rapids. 1979. p.561
2. For Bultmann's views, see, e.g., his *Primitive Christianity in its Contemporary Setting*. Trans. by R. H. Fuller. Edinburgh. 1960.
3. For a useful survey of the available material, see E. M. Yamauchi. *Pre-Christian Gnosticism: A Survey of the Proposed Evidences*. Grand Rapids. 1973.
4. The issue is well discussed by P. T. O'Brien. *Colossians, Philemon*. Word Biblical Commentary. Waco, Texas. 1982. pp. xlix -liii
5. W. G. de Burgh. *Legacy of the Ancient World*. 2nd. edn. revised and enlarged. London. 1947
6. For fuller information on the background to Paul, see Bo Reicke. *The New Testament Era: The World of the Bible from 500 B.C. to A.D.100*. Translated by D. E. Green. London. 1968.

3

The Damascus Road

If you have examined the Contents Page of this book, you may have noticed that, with this one exception, there are no chapters on the life of Paul. This is because a chronological account of his life does not fall within its main purpose. There are in fact good books on Paul's life on the market already.[1]

There is however one event in his life we must consider very carefully. This is his encounter with the living Christ on the road from Jerusalem to Damascus. It affected everything in his life from that time on.

Record and Reflection

Where can we learn about it? In the Acts of the Apostles. Here there are no less than three accounts, one by Luke the narrator (in Acts 9) and two by Paul himself as he gave his witness for Christ in two quite different situations (in Acts 22 and 26). This means, in fact, that Luke emphasizes Paul's conversion as much as he does that of Cornelius and his friends, for he gives three accounts of that event also, one by himself as the narrator (Acts 10) and the other two from the lips of Peter (Acts 11 and 15).

This is interesting, especially as Luke was a Gentile. These were the two events in the story of the early church which were of the greatest significance for the evangelization of the Gentile world.

What though about Paul's letters? There are thirteen

claiming to be his, eighty-seven chapters in all. Surely if that meeting with Jesus on the Damascus Road was such a big, life-changing experience for him, we would expect him to mention it frequently!

Surprisingly, he makes very few express references to it. Don't forget though that two of the Acts accounts are actually from Paul's own lips. There are no detailed reports of it in the letters, but we do find a few brief but significant references.

In Galatians 1:15,16, he says, 'God, who set me apart from birth and called me by his grace, was pleased to reveal his Son in me so that I might preach him among the Gentiles.' As we read these words, his deep sense of gratitude comes across.

In 1 Corinthians 9:1, he asks, 'Am I not free? Am I not an apostle? Have I not seen Jesus our Lord?' Again we can hardly miss the emotional tone of these words.

This is true also in 1 Corinthians 15:8-10. Here he has been giving a catalogue of the resurrection appearances of Jesus, and, at the end of them, he says, 'last of all he appeared to me also, as to one abnormally born,' and follows this by declaring, 'For I am the least of the apostles and do not even deserve to be called an apostle, because I persecuted the church of God. But by the grace of God I am what I am.'

These passages and their deeply felt comments are impressive, but is there no more than this? Probably there is. What about a verse like 2 Corinthians 4:6?

All the records of Paul's conversion in Acts emphasize light. Christ appeared in a blaze of light and that glory shone, not only on Paul's pathway but within him, as he says in Galatians 1:16.

The same theme of light and glory dominates much of

2 Corinthians chapter 3 and the opening verses of chapter 4. Paul writes here about the great difference made when the veil of unbelief is taken away from the heart of a Jew. It is then that the light gets through.

He goes on to say, in verses 5 and 6, 'For we do not preach ourselves, but Jesus Christ as Lord, and ourselves as your servants for Jesus' sake. For God, who said, "Let light shine out of darkness," made his light shine in our hearts to give us the light of the knowledge of the glory of God in the face of Christ.'

Here Paul is thinking about his role as a preacher of the gospel of Christ's glory. What then could be more natural than for his mind to turn to the great event in which he was commissioned to proclaim this message?

His reference to the face of Christ and to a light shining in the heart makes it seem very likely that as he wrote he was standing in his imagination on the road where the risen Christ appeared to him. He could find no more satisfactory analogy for it than a very great one indeed, the blaze of light which pierced the cosmic darkness when God said, 'Let there be light'. God's light in Christ had pierced the inner darkness of Paul's heart.

Then, in chapter 5:14-18, he is still preoccupied with his role as a preacher of the good news of Jesus, and he says that Christ's love had great motivating force for him, and that it had completely changed his outlook on people.

This new attitude began, of course, when he saw Christ himself on that Damascus Road. Verse 17 looks as if it is based on a vivid memory, if not of the Damascus Road itself, at least of the restoration of his sight a few days later. We will insert a word which the NIV has omitted, 'Therefore, if anyone is in Christ, he is a new creation; the old has

gone, (behold) the new has come!' Can you sense here
something of Paul's amazed surprise at the new light that
had come to him through Christ?

Why was not Paul more explicit? Perhaps there is a clue
to this in 2 Corinthians 10-13. If you read these chapters
through, you will notice that at point after point he shows his
embarrassment at the fact that he had to 'boast' so much. It
looks as if reference to his personal experiences was not
congenial to him. He much preferred to put the emphasis on
Christ himself. As he says, 'we do not preach ourselves, but
Jesus Christ as Lord' (2 Corinthians 4:5).

There is something else though. It is more than possible
that Paul's references to his apostleship, even his very use of
the word, 'apostle,' may often have brought back the Damascus Road event to his mind. This is because it was at that time
the risen Christ commissioned him to be an apostle.

If you read again the passages in Galatians 1 and 1
Corinthians 9 and 15 where he does refer to this experience,
you will see that in each of them he is writing quite
specifically about his apostleship.

Yes, we do have to go to Acts for the actual historical
facts, but there is clear evidence in Paul's letters that
meeting the living Christ on that occasion meant a great deal
to him.

Objective and Subjective

What was it that happened at that time? Was it a purely
subjective experience, something that existed only within
Paul's imaginative faculty, as in a dream or trance?

Paul certainly believed that he encountered the actual
risen Christ, not an apparition of him.

We have some unexpected confirmatory evidence of

the objective character of this experience. This is to be found in the very difficulties we encounter in trying to harmonize Luke's three accounts. It can be done, but it is not easy. We have to work at it.

In this respect these three accounts are rather like the difficulties of reconciling all the details of the first Easter Sunday as these are given in the Four Gospels. There was no attempt to standardise the story, as there might well have been in both cases if it had lacked an objective reference. When the evidence of law court witnesses is extremely easy to harmonise, it may raise questions about possible collusion between them.

As we get to grips with the details given, it seems in fact that the men who travelled with Paul were aware of an objective happening of some sort. They saw a light and they heard a sound. They did not however see Jesus himself as Paul did, nor did they hear his voice. So the experience was a much more personal one for him than for them.

This is surely in accordance with what Paul says in Galatians 1:16. The Greek word translated here as 'in' by the NIV really means 'into'. This means then that the glory, the objective light on the roadway, which came from the risen Christ himself, had its subjective counterpart in an inward revelation. In other words, by the grace of God, it was both the outer and the inner eyes of Paul that now saw Jesus clearly.

This means, of course, that there is something we need to say and to say clearly. We cannot use Paul's experience as a complete paradigm for a conversion experience today. There are many people who are looking for something as dramatic as this, when it may not be God's plan to deal with them in this way.

The essence of a conversion experience is a clear understanding of who Christ is and what he has done to save us, and a commitment of the will to him in penitent faith. This may happen in a dramatic moment but it may not. We must not confuse the essence of an experience with its accompanying circumstances.

There can be little doubt that Paul was affected in every aspect of his being. The temporary blindness, although perhaps symbolic, was also physically actual. His love for Christ appears clearly in all his writings. Moreover, as we shall see, his conversion had a profound intellectual effect on him.

Conversion and Commissioning

Anyone who has followed the books on Paul that have come out over the past two or three decades will have noticed a gradual change in the attitude of many writers to Paul's Damascus Road experience.

What has happened? The emphasis has been taken off conversion and transferred to call or commissioning.

Why this change? It could in part be due to an increased desire to bridge the gap between Jews and Christians, and so to play down the element of conversion. It is often said that a Hebrew Christian has not been so much converted as completed.

Now undoubtedly there is truth in the positive side of this, for if a Jew has come to his true Messiah this is the fulfilment of all he was meant to be. Yet it is neither wise nor Biblical to play down the term 'conversion' altogether. If a nominal Christian needs to make a personal commitment to Christ this is surely true also of a Jew!

There is however another reason. This is the increasing

interest of New Testament scholars in Paul's apostleship, and especially his conviction that he was called to be the apostle of the Gentiles. This comes out in books by scholars like Johannes Munck[2], E. P. Sanders[3] and others.

There is one thing of which we can be quite sure. Paul's Christian consciousness and his apostolic awareness were linked with each other most intimately. No doubt they could be distinguished but we cannot separate them. They both take their rise from one great experience.

What in fact is conversion if it is not a surrender of a once rebellious will to a new Master? It is a most serious mistake to view it as a purely emotional or intellectual experience. It is essentially volitional, although of course it will involve both the feelings and the mind. Anything less than this is not really a conversion at all.

Certainly then we should continue to speak of Paul's conversion but to see it essentially as a radical commitment to the Lordship of Christ, who in fact called him at that time to the apostolic task.

Before and After

One of the issues which is in view in this debate about the nature of the Damascus Road experience is connected with the interpretation of Romans 7.

Until comparatively recent years, most discussion of this has revolved around the question as to whether, in this chapter, Paul is writing about his pre- or post-conversion experience. Now however the main question is whether he is really writing about himself at all.

At one time it was taken almost for granted that much of this chapter was autobiographical, but not now. W. G. Kümmel has argued that the context of Romans 7 in Paul's letter requires us to understand that he is here defending the Law, not recounting his personal experience. He also maintained that Rabbinic convention would not allow Paul to use the first personal pronoun for this purpose. At most, he can only have been describing his own experience if he regarded it as generally representative [4]. Also Paul has used the first personal pronoun earlier in the same epistle (3:7) to present somebody else's argument. Many New Testament scholars have been convinced by Kümmel's arguments.

It is now being said that the whole interpretation of this passage was taken in a wrong direction by Luther. The reformer, somewhat following Augustine, viewed it in the light of the troubled conscience he himself had when the Holy Spirit convicted him of his sins.

Did Paul have a troubled conscience before his conversion? According to Kümmel, the autobiographical sections of Galatians 1 and Philippians 3 give us no evidence for this, and Acts 26:14 ('It is hard for you to kick against the goads') has no reference at all to a disturbed conscience but rather to the fact that his opposition to Christianity was senseless and fruitless.

It must be said that not all Pauline scholars have gone over to Kümmel's point of view, although a substantial number of them have. We will look at the matter more fully later.

The term 'paradigm shift' is a modern one. It was coined by a philosopher of science, Thomas Kuhn, and a number of other writers have taken it up. It refers to a major reorientation in somebody's whole outlook on some matter of importance.

It may even affect the whole of society. It takes place, for example, whenever there is a major shift of perspective in the scientific world. So, people like Copernicus, Galileo,

Newton and Einstein have been associated with major changes in cosmology, and these have deeply affected the outlook of society in general.

In the individual, it may go even deeper than this, so that his entire inner life as well as his understanding of the external world may undergo reorientation.

This certainly happened in the case of Saul of Tarsus. From the Damascus Road onwards, Christ dominated his whole outlook. He was Christ's man, and this meant not only that his affections were moved towards Christ and that his will was now committed to Christ's will. It meant too that his thinking underwent a radical change. What exactly that was we will try to see in the next chapter.

Maybe, as we have indicated above, Paul's experience on the Damascus Road is not intended to be an exact pattern for others, but the essential spiritual core of it is. Conversion is not treated in the New Testament as a kind of optional extra. Christ as Divine Lord rightly demands our submission and Christ as Saviour graciously woos us as we see the depth of his love revealed at the cross.

He calls for the submission of our wills to him and to his sovereign and loving purpose. We can give him nothing more. We dare give him no less.

References

1. A useful book on both the life and the epistles of Paul is F. F. Bruce. *Paul, Apostle of the Heart set Free*. Exeter. 1977.

2. J. Munck. *Paul and the Salvation of Mankind*. London. 1959.

3. E. P. Sanders. *Paul and Palestinian Judaism: a comparison of patterns of religion*. London. 1977

4. Kümmel's basic work on this is *Romer 7 und die Bekehrung des Paulus*. Leipzig. 1929. repr. Munich. 1974

4

Gripped by the Gospel

One word constantly recurs in Paul's letters, almost like some 'magnificent obsession'. Here is the major key to his work and not only so, for it unlocks our understanding of his whole lifestyle after he met the risen Christ. That word is 'gospel', 'good news'.

Study the times he uses it and you will find it far outnumbers its occurrences elsewhere in the New Testament. He employs *euangelion* ('gospel') sixty times, while it is found only sixteen times in the rest of the New Testament. There is in fact only one occurrence in a letter not written by him (1 Peter 4:17).

This disproportion, although not quite so marked, also applies to its companion verb *euangelizomai*. Luke comes second for his use of *euangelizomai*.

These facts become even more impressive when we remember that Luke was a companion of Paul. Work for years with somebody you admire and you will probably find yourself using some of that person's favourite words. Even the use of the verb in 1 Peter may not be free of Paul's influence, for it has often been remarked that this letter's vocabulary is rather like Paul's. This is not surprising in view of 1 Peter 5:12, where Peter says, 'With the help of Silas ... I have written to you briefly.' Do you remember Silas, Paul's missionary companion?

Spinoza, the Dutch philosopher, was described as 'a

God-intoxicated man'. With more justification, Paul might be described as 'a gospel-intoxicated man', except that intoxication often dulls the mind while Paul's preoccupation with the gospel actually freed and sharpened his.

Let us stay with this fact for a while. Understand the gospel and what it meant for Paul and you will find this banishes all caricatures of his outlook.

Caricature, whether in the form of drawings or verbal descriptions, is all too easy if you are dealing with people who have strong opinions. That is why caricaturists so often concentrate on politicians. It can also be applied to religious leaders, for they too tend to have strong views.

What caricatures of Paul have appeared in modern times! He has been represented as a woman-hater, as an ungracious and contentious person, as a martinet in discipline, as an arrogant leader. In fact, all these images are eccentric in the true sense of that term, for they depart from the centre. They ignore the fact that to him what mattered most was the gospel.

You see, the gospel is so positive and *Christ-centred*. It is about God accepting us despite all our demerits and because of Christ. He accepts us because Christ died for our sins and was raised from the dead.

So then Jesus Christ is the heart of the gospel. This means that when we say Paul was a gospel-centred man we are really saying he was a Christ-centred man. It was in fact the Damascus Road encounter with Christ that set his heart ablaze with the gospel.

Now if the gospel is Christ-centred it is of course *doctrinal*. It has important theological content.

Paul sets out the essence of the gospel in 1 Corinthians 15:3-4. Here we see it to be centred in the death, burial and resurrection of Christ, not simply as historical events (important though their historicity is), but in those events interpreted in accordance with Old Testament Scripture.

The arch-persecutor of the Christians could now see very plainly that his conception of the Messiah had been all wrong. As a Pharisee he would have held the Messiah to be a very great man but no more, and that his role would be that of a triumphant warrior-king.

He now saw, not simply that suffering was an element in the life of the Messiah (not in itself the main issue), but that it was absolutely central to his work. He began very clearly to hear the Messianic melody in a minor key (he suffered on the cross), which is at the same time a higher key (for Jesus is Lord).

'Christ,' says Paul, 'died for our sins' (1 Cor. 15:3). This means that the gospel has implications for what we believe, not only about God but also about human beings. Bultmann may have been wrong in taking all his theology back to anthropology, the doctrine of man, but obviously what Paul believed about God's solution must relate to what he believed about man's predicament.

What then was the human predicament? Nowhere does Paul deal with this more fully than in Romans 1:18-3:21. A superficial reading may give the reader the impression that the subject of this passage is sin. In actual fact, it is much more about God's judgement on human sin.

To fail to realise this is to leave oneself open, for instance, to the idea that 'expiation' is an adequate translation of *hilasterion* in Romans 3:25. The word 'expiation' views sin as needing to be dealt with, which is true. The stronger translation 'propitiation', however, includes that but goes beyond it to the fact that God's wrath is turned away from the sinner, and so it recognises the strong emphasis on God's wrath and judgement in the context. 'Propitiation' sees sin not only as alienating the sinner from God but alienating God from the sinner.

How wonderful then to find Paul saying, about Christ, that 'God presented him as the one who would turn aside his wrath, taking away sin' (NIV margin)! Paul saw clearly not only that this is the Saviour we need but also that he is the one God has actually provided in his grace.

The gospel is also *challenging*. It may seem at times that Paul's gospel was essentially a set of truths to accept. This is however a serious misunderstanding of it.

The gospel, as we have seen, has very important theological content. We are called to accept its truth, for it is God's truth. This engagement of our intellects with it is not, however, enough.

Study Paul's sermons in Acts and you will find that he was not concerned only with the objective content of the gospel, but also with its subjective appropriation and response. In other words, he calls for repentance and faith.

We must however be careful not to retreat from intellectualism into subjectivism. Paul would have been most unhappy with an approach to the Christian faith that put all the stress on the individual's experience. His Christianity was a response to a message and that message was centred in Christ crucified and risen.

For him, the gospel was *personal*. Three times (in Romans 2:16; 16:25; 2 Timothy 2:8) he uses the term 'my gospel'. As we shall see, this does not mean he saw it as his invention nor as his own personal property to be jealously guarded from use by others. Far from it. Nothing delighted him more than to find that others were also declaring this good news. But the gospel was so bound up with his life and calling in Christ that he could use this expression of it most aptly.

It was his because it had touched his own life, transforming it. Life without the Christ of the gospel now became unthinkable, for, as he wrote to the Philippians, 'to me, to live is Christ' (Phil. 1:21).

It was his also in the sense that Christ gave it to him as a sacred trust. It was a precious possession, to be communicated faithfully and fully. This he did wherever he went on his extensive journeys throughout the Mediterranean world.

For him, too, the gospel was *corporate*. He rarely proclaimed it as a solitary evangelist. Nearly always he had others with him. When using the term 'our gospel' (1 Thess. 1:5; 2 Thess. 2:14), he links Silas and Timothy with him as they are associated with him at the beginning of each of these letters. In 2 Corinthians 4:3, his association is with Timothy, as a glance at the opening of the letter will make clear.

It might be argued, of course, that Silas and Timothy were so closely identified with him that they were bound to agree with his outlook, and that Paul's view could still be somewhat idiosyncratic. But we must set against this Paul's strong conviction that the gospel was also *apostolic*.

Certainly, as he is at pains to show in the first two chapters of Galatians, Paul did not gain his gospel from the other apostles. He also makes it quite clear there, nevertheless, that he and they were in total harmony about it.

1 Corinthians 15 confirms this. There he declares not only the central importance of the cross and resurrection of Jesus and the theological meaning of these great events, but also his absolute unity with the other apostles on this. The

Corinthian Christians could of course check this very easily, as there was a Peter (Cephas) party among them.

But wasn't there a clash between Paul and Peter at Antioch? Yes, but what was it actually about?

Paul tells us. 'When Peter came to Antioch, I opposed him to his face, because he was clearly in the wrong. Before certain men came from James, he used to eat with the Gentiles. But when they arrived, he began to draw back and separate himself from the Gentiles because he was afraid of those who belonged to the circumcision group. The other Jews joined him in his hypocrisy, so that by their hypocrisy even Barnabas was led astray. When I saw that they were not acting in line with the truth of the gospel, I said to Peter in front of them all ...' (Gal. 2:11-14).

Do you see what was at issue here? Peter was not acting from conviction but from fear and so in fact he was out of line with the gospel which both he and Paul believed. So the incident had nothing whatever to do with the content or nature of the gospel, but simply with how it should affect our practice. The evidence of 1 Corinthians 15, as well as of Galatians 2:6-10, that these two apostles held to and proclaimed the same gospel, is unaffected by this.

Then his gospel was also *Dominical*, that is it was from the Lord himself. He goes to a lot of trouble to make this clear, especially in Galatians but also in 1 Corinthians. It was not of human but of divine origin. It was given to him by the risen Christ.

It was also dominical in the sense that it accorded completely with the teaching of Jesus during his earthly ministry.

This has in fact often been denied. During the heyday of Liberalism, and especially in the period when Albrecht

Ritschl's teaching dominated a great deal of New Testament scholarship (at the end of the 19th Century and the beginning of the 20th), a wedge was driven between the teaching of Jesus and that of Paul.

Happily there has been a swing away from this. There is much less tendency now to see such a radical difference between Paul's teaching and his Lord's, or to see Paul transforming the 'simple teaching of Jesus' into a theologized message about judgement and salvation. There is no doubt that C. H. Dodd's work, *The Apostolic Preaching and its Developments*, published in 1936, exerted a major influence as far as this is concerned. Dodd argued that one essential gospel runs right through the New Testament and binds it all together.

It is true that Dodd's view has been questioned, at least in part, more recently by those who see some diversity of gospel in the New Testament documents.[1] Even so, there has been no major retreat to the late 19th century view of an essential disharmony between the gospel of Jesus and that of Paul.

Certainly there is difference of terminology, but the nature of Jesus and also the necessity for his death are leading themes in the way the teaching of Jesus is presented. This is true in all the gospel traditions, including the Johannine.

Because the gospel is God's own revelation and represents the only way of salvation for sinners, it is completely *non-negotiable*.

On some issues Paul was surprisingly tolerant. He dealt with churches which had all kinds of problems. In some of them the standard of Christian living was low and there were all kinds of theological aberrations. Even in his letters to such churches, however, Paul gives thanks for the Christians in them.

There is however one exception. The Letter to the Galatians contains no such thanksgiving. Not only so, but Paul moves straight in with major criticism of the Galatian churches. When we see what this criticism is, we can understand the severe tone of that letter: 'I am astonished that you are so quickly deserting the one who called you by the grace of Christ and are turning to a different gospel - which is really no gospel at all' (Gal. 1:6,7).

The Galatians were in danger of surrendering the very gospel itself. Paul goes so far as to say that if even an angel were to preach a different gospel from the one he had himself proclaimed in Galatia, he should suffer the divine curse (Gal. 1:8).

If the gospel was non-negotiable for Paul, it should certainly be so for modern-day Christians. Never can its truth, its centrality, its absolute necessity, be surrendered, no matter what arguments for this may be put forward.

Now a point of quite major importance for the theme of this book is that for Paul the gospel was *determinative* and *regulative*.

A study of his life and letters shows us that he had many problems to face and important decisions to make. What were the decisive factors for him in making decisions, especially those which did not affect him alone but also the infant churches for which he had a responsibility?

The obvious answer is 'the Holy Spirit'. Yes, of course it was the Holy Spirit, but this is only a partial answer. It still leaves open the question as to the means used by the Spirit to convey this guidance to Paul.

When he had a problem Paul undoubtedly consulted the

Scriptures, the Old Testament writings which were the Bible for his day. These Scriptures he interpreted in the light of the gospel.

What happened if the Old Testament did not provide guidance? On such occasions Paul wrestled with the big issue in the light of the gospel itself.

So then the gospel was basic to everything, to the way he interpreted the Old Testament, to theological questions, to social and ecclesiastical questions, to personal problems. Everything, just everything, was to be viewed in its light.

Now if this is true, it is enormously helpful to modern Christians and especially to church leaders, when they too are faced with problems.

Of course, we accept the regulative function of the Scriptures and these now embrace the New Testament writings, including Paul's own epistles. But suppose there are problems for which no explicit guidance is given in Scripture? If we find such problems, then surely for us the answer is to face and tackle them in the light of the gospel.

We will find plenty of examples to illustrate this very important point as we move through the various chapters of this book.

It is, of course, most important for us to ask ourselves in the presence of God if we are as committed to the gospel as Paul was, and also whether like him we allow it to affect every part of our thinking and, more than that, every part of our lives?

References
1. See especially J. D. G. Dunn. *Unity and Diversity in the New Testament. An Inquiry into the Character of Earliest Christianity.* London. 1977

5

Paul and the Law

When Saul of Tarsus set out to persecute the Christians, he was a dedicated Pharisee. When he emerged from the Damascus Road experience, he was a dedicated Christian.

This was a spiritual revolution, but it also affected his theology. Was it a total change of outlook? How much re-thinking would he have to do?

The Pharisees of New Testament times

We meet these people quite frequently in the gospels. Clearly their outlook was very different from that of Jesus. He had frequent clashes with them.

It might therefore surprise some readers of this book to know that theologically the Pharisees were much closer to Jesus than the other two main Jewish sects of New Testament times, the Sadducees and the Essenes. If, for instance, they had talked with him about such subjects as the resurrection of the dead or the ministry of angels, there would have been a lot of common ground.

Why then were there so many clashes? Because the issues on which they did differ were of such enormous importance.

If you are a Christian and you were to meet somebody who told you Jesus Christ was simply a very great man and not God and that your personal salvation could never be based on what he has done for you on the cross but on your

49

own efforts to keep the Law of God, wouldn't you find yourself in disagreement with him?

Differences about the person and work of Jesus and about the basis of personal salvation can never be side issues but always central ones.

But do Christians today have a true picture of Pharisaism as it was in New Testament times? As we have seen already, some modern writers, following E. P. Sanders [1], would query this. They object to the way Christians have so often thought of the Judaism of the New Testament period as dominated by legalism.

What is the basis for these accusations of Christian prejudice against the Pharisees? A study of the written works of the Pharisees themselves. From these some scholars have concluded that 1st Century Pharisees laid rather more emphasis on the grace of God than the New Testament writers appear to have given them credit for.

Without doubt the work of Sanders has had a major influence on subsequent writers, many of whom start from the assumption that he has completely made his case. Certainly his arguments aimed at a corrective have positive value, but has he over-stated his case? [2]

The teaching of our Lord recorded in Matthew 23 undoubtedly presents in some detail a picture of the Pharisees with whom he came into contact at the local synagogues, and he saw them as legalists. Surely we must take this seriously!

Is it possible then that the writings of the great teachers among the Pharisees, those writings which are the basis of Sanders' views, were one thing and the oral instruction given at local level something else?

Sanders does not say much about the Gospels, but he

himself admits that 'the possibility cannot be completely excluded that there were Jews accurately hit by the polemic of Matthew 23, who attended only to trivia and neglected the weightier matters. Human nature being what it is, one supposes that there were some such. One must say, however, that the surviving Jewish literature does not reveal them.' [3]

Possibly, but the New Testament writers, and especially the four evangelists, do. All four Gospel writers saw the Pharisees as legalists.

Even Luke? It might seem at first that his estimate of them must be a little different. After all, in his second volume, he tells us that the great Gamaliel called on others to be open-minded about Christianity (Acts 5:33-40), at least for the time being. Also Luke shows us Paul, in a personal crisis, getting some support from the Pharisees against the Sadducees (Acts 23:6-10).

Do not forget though that Luke, just as much as the other Gospel writers, shows Jesus in frequent conflict with the Pharisees during his ministry. The two incidents in Acts should encourage us to take this evidence from his Gospel very seriously indeed, for they demonstrate his historical honesty. He was not out either to blacken or to whitewash the Pharisees, but simply to tell the truth.

One of the effects of sin is that it blinds us to the way things really are. We can easily become legalists and imagine we can do something to make ourselves right with God. The truth is, of course, that there is nothing we can offer God that is not completely unacceptable because of our sin.

Look at it this way. The New Testament makes it abundantly clear that there is only one way of salvation.

This is by God's grace and through faith in Christ. Certainly it is not by anything we can do. Despite this, there are many today who profess to be Christians and yet imagine they can be saved by their works. Is it not more than likely then that this kind of legalistic outlook was also present among the Jews of New Testament times?

Among their local leaders and teachers too? Yes! Un-happily, it is not unknown even for Christian ministers to preach in such a way that the grace of God in the gospel is seriously obscured.

Even if the major writers among the Pharisees put some emphasis on the grace of God, most of the contacts of Jesus with Pharisees (until the final stage of his life) were with those from the local synagogues in Galilee. The teachers in these may well have played down grace and played up duty, and they may have done this more than those in Jerusalem.

Certainly the Jerusalem Pharisees came down to investi-gate and they had some very strong things to say against him, but they were probably influenced by the attitude of the Galilean Pharisees (Mark 3:22-30). Of course, the Sanhe-drin, the Great Council of the Jews, that eventually condemned him to death, contained both Pharisees and Sadducees.

At least two of the Pharisees at Jerusalem, Nicodemus and Joseph of Arimathaea, were secret disciples (Luke 23:50-53; John 19:38-42). Could there have been others?

Remember too that the very earliest Christians, people like Peter and John, were reared in the synagogues of Galilee where the Pharisees taught week in, week out. Apart from home training, this is where they got their understand-ing of religion before they met Jesus. They can certainly be trusted to know what, *in practice*, the outlook of the Galilee Pharisees was at this time.

More than this, we need to remember that our Lord himself must have had extensive experience of synagogue theology and practice as a child and even as an adult in the years before his ministry began.

Are we really prepared to say that the Gospel writers all presented a caricature of the Pharisees that was untrue to the facts? Are we prepared to say, further, that Jewish disciples of Jesus passed on a view of the Pharisees that they must have known to be false? Most of all, are we prepared to say either that they falsified the stories of the clashes between Jesus and the Pharisees or even that Jesus was himself a party to such a misrepresentation?

In this book we will take the portrayal of Pharisaism in the Gospels with the seriousness it deserves.

Saul the Pharisee

We embarked on this brief study of New Testament Pharisaism because we are interested in the extent to which Paul's outlook must have altered as a result of his life-changing encounter with the living Christ.

But, it may be objected, Paul was not a mere local synagogue elder. In fact, he was not a Palestinian Pharisee at all, but a Pharisee of the Dispersion, born in a foreign land.

Yes, but he spent a very important part of his life in the Holy Land, instructed by Gamaliel, probably the greatest Pharisee of that time. Gamaliel was not a hardliner but was a distinguished member of a group that was known to have a slightly less rigid approach to the application of the Law than some others.

How legalistic then was Paul himself before his conversion? We can find the answer to this question from the man himself.

On his last visit to Jerusalem, he had the chance of speaking to a great crowd of Jews. This is what he said: 'Under Gamaliel I was thoroughly trained in the law of our fathers and was just as zealous for God as any of you are today' (Acts 22:3).

Does he mean that his zeal for God took the form of legalism? It would certainly seem so, for he writes to the Galatians of being 'extremely zealous for the traditions of my fathers' (Gal. 1:14). This means that, like the Pharisees generally, he was concerned to promote the oral as well as the written law.

His letters were written in the context of his evangelistic, church-planting and pastoral work, but, as we have seen, when he spoke or wrote about Jewish legalism, he knew this not only from contact with Jews as a Christian, but from his own experience.

In Romans 7:7-25, Paul writes about a man's experience of the law, of sinful failure and of inner struggle. What are we to make of this passage?

In verses 7 to 13, the person concerned becomes aware of God's law against covetousness, and his consequent sin brings death to him. In verses 14 to 25, he discovers that for him principle and performance do not match. He so wants to do God's will in the Law but he fails. There is something evil inside him. It is Christ who rescues him.

Who is this man? Is he a Pharisee throughout the passage, with his conversion to Christ coming at its end? Or could verses 7 to 13 instead be a description of Adam's fall into sin?

These verses are certainly about a man without Christ, but what about verses 14 to 25? Does an unconverted man really desire to keep God's law with the intensity shown in this passage? If the passage does describe Christian experience, has Paul deliberately reserved his exposition of our spiritual resources until the next chapter to emphasize our dependence on Christ through the Spirit?

There is no general agreement as to the answers to many of these questions. To deal with them in detail would take us too far from our main subject here, but you will find that all the major commentators discuss them.

For us just now the main question is a further one. The passage is written in the first person singular. Is Paul then writing about himself?

It used to be taken for granted by most commentators that he is. The account is so vivid and its portrayal of a man at war within himself seems so heartfelt, that most readers would take it for granted they are reading autobiography.

As we have seen, however, there has been a change of outlook among the scholars. Is it really an important issue?

Its importance can be exaggerated. Even if it is a representative rather than a personal description, it certainly includes Paul.

This means then that he knew in personal experience how strong the pull to covetousness was, in contravention of God's commandment. Also we can say that if, as many think, verses 14 to 25 describe moral struggle after Christian conversion, this serves to underline even more strongly how utterly impossible it is for the non-Christian to save himself.

What then are we to make of Philippians 3:6, where, in an account of his former confidence in the flesh, he says, 'as for legalistic righteousness, faultless'?

The way Paul phrases his thought here suggests that he had in view outward conformity to the law, for legalism focuses on the outward. Moreover, this phrase is preceded by the words, 'as for zeal, persecuting the church'. After his conversion Paul saw this persecuting zeal to be deeply sinful. Whatever he had been earlier, the man confronted by the risen Christ on the Damascus Road was a violent and blasphemous persecutor (1 Tim. 1:13).

Paul's awareness of the impossibility of self-salvation was highly relevant to his evangelistic work. Most of this work was not in the Holy Land but in the Gentile lands of the Mediterranean world. If anything, Jews living in Gentile lands were more rather than less legalistic than those in Palestine. They laid great emphasis on the keeping of the Sabbath and on the food laws. As we have seen, it was these things that most clearly differentiated the Jew from the Gentile in such places.

So wherever Paul went he proclaimed that we cannot be saved by our own efforts, including the Jew's strenuous attempts to save himself by keeping the Law of Moses. What the law was powerless to do, because it was weakened by the sinful nature, God did - in Christ (Rom. 8:3).

The Old Testament: Law-centred or Christ-centred?
Paul makes a very large number of references to the Old Testament. It is impossible for us to examine them all, but it is clear his understanding of it was thoroughly Christian. He saw it witnessing to Christ in all sorts of ways.

For instance, in his letter to the Romans, he indicates that Jesus Christ is of the seed of David (Rom 1:3), that he was not only the Root of Jesse (Rom. 15:12; cf. Isa. 11:10) but also the Stone over whom Israel stumbled because they did not trust in him (Rom. 9:33; cf. Isa. 8:14; 28:16)

Now this new understanding of the ancient scriptures

probably did not come to him in a sudden flash of inspiration. At the time of his encounter with the living Christ, or shortly afterwards, he must have seen that Jesus is in fact the key to the Old Testament. The implications of this are, however, so far-reaching, that they cannot all have come home to him at once.

Either at once, or over a period, his approach to the Old Testament would become thoroughly Christ-centred rather than Law-centred. Without doubt this was already true in the earliest letters we have from his pen. We can be sure too that the Scriptures came alight with increasing meaning in the context of his actual ministry.

Legalism at Galatia

The whole issue came to stark prominence and importance, of course, when he found himself dealing with Jewish Christians still infected by Pharisaism. Some of these folk were promoting a legalistic approach to the Christian faith.

These were in Antioch (Acts 15:1ff.) and also in Galatia. We know too from the Pastoral Epistles (the letters to Timothy and Titus) that this type of teaching was a continuing problem throughout much of his ministry (1 Tim. 1:6-11; Titus 1: 10-16; 3:9).

The false teachers at Galatia appear to have used three arguments, biographical, theological and ethical. Paul deals with each of these in turn.

Their first argument was that Paul was not a true apostle but simply an emissary of the original apostles of Jesus centred in Jerusalem. He had in fact gone beyond his brief in preaching a gospel of free salvation to the Galatians.

Secondly, they declared that, although it was true Christ had given his life for the salvation of sinners, circumcision and Law-keeping were essential if they were to benefit from his saving work. This was because only in this way could they become children of Abraham, to whom the promises of God had originally been given.

Finally, they seem to have argued that the discipline of the Law was necessary in order to curb human sin. They probably appealed to the continuing awareness of the power of sin which the Galatians will have had.

How then did Paul handle this issue? He dealt with it fairly and squarely by treating the arguments seriously and answering them one by one. In other words, he engaged in a kind of apologetics directed not to those outside but those inside the church.

In the first two chapters of his letter to the Galatians he gave an account of his life as a Christian and showed that he had been commissioned directly by the risen Christ to be an apostle. He had not received his gospel from the other apostles but rather from the Lord himself. Not only so, but the other apostles gave complete recognition to the authenticity of his understanding of the gospel.

He then went on in chapters 3 and 4 to deal with the theological argument. It is true that the promises of God were given to Abraham and his children, so that we need to become his children to inherit them, but who in fact are the children of Abraham? They are those who share his faith. This he demonstrated from the pages of the Old Testament.

In terms of the ethical argument, he showed that it is not reliance on the Law which counters the power of sin, but the Spirit of God in the hearts of Christian believers, and that it is not circumcision but faith that works by love which produces the God-honouring fruits of righteousness.

Here then was a major theological problem with practical implications. It mattered a great deal that the Galatians should not seek circumcision in a legalistic spirit. Paul confronts the issue theologically, answering the main arguments frankly and directly.

This can be a guide to us. If a problem is essentially theological there can be no substitute for giving it theological treatment.

In recent decades, for instance, many churches have been split over issues concerning the work of the Holy Spirit. Some church leaders have dealt with this purely at a pastoral level, seeking to help concerned and troubled individuals. This of course needs to be done, but it is vital that the matter should be treated theologically, and clear and definite Biblical teaching given.

Legalism today
The Galatian heresy of course cut at the very roots of the gospel of grace. This kind of problem is by no means confined to the New Testament period. There is plenty of evidence from the following centuries that Pauline teaching on this subject was often misunderstood or virtually ignored.

In the late Middle Ages, many believed the sacraments to be saving ordinances in themselves. Not only so but they were essential to salvation. We should remember too that, for the church of the time, these included not only Baptism and the Lord's Supper, but several others, including penance.

Luther found immense relief when he began to see, through Paul's writings, that the just live by faith and not by meritorious works. This great relief finds its explanation in his former adherence to a legalistic form of Christianity.

Classic Seventh-Day Adventism has also promoted legalism and has taught that those who do not observe the Sabbath on the seventh day of the week have the mark of the beast. It is good to know that many in Adventism are now seeking an approach more in line with Paul's emphasis on grace [4]. But mainline Protestant churches too can promote legalism without realising it. Many who have a link with paedo-baptist churches tend to rely on their baptism as children, while those who practise believers' baptism can easily give the impression that this is necessary for salvation. It is important for the issue to be raised quite explicitly and dealt with in the teaching programme of a local church.

What about counselling? Major evangelists have trained local Christians to act as counsellors during their crusades and many local churches have followed suit, using counsellors they have themselves trained to deal with enquirers.

Such moves are to be welcomed, so long as the counsellors themselves are able to teach clearly, at individual level, the totally gracious basis of personal salvation.

Of course, it would be a mistake to think that all that is needed is clear teaching.

A well-known Bible teacher was preaching as a visitor in a local church in Scotland. In his sermon, he took great pains to explain that God accepts us, not on the basis of any merit of our own, but entirely on the basis of Christ's merits and his death in our place.

At the close of the service a lady spoke to him at the door, thanking him warmly for what he had said. He talked with her, and discovered to his astonishment that she had totally misunderstood his sermon and imagined it was simply confirming her endeavours to save herself!

At a crucial stage in the development of the early church,

the apostles said they would give themselves to prayer and to the ministry of the word (Acts 6:4).

We need to notice the combination. Satan is at work blinding the minds of unbelievers. The truth must be proclaimed, but it is vital also to pray for the Holy Spirit to work through the word to dispel the darkness and bring the light of the gospel into people's hearts.

References
1. See especially E. P. Sanders. *Paul and Palestinian Judaism.* London. 1977
2. Criticisms of Sanders' thesis are included in S. Westerholm. *Israel's Law and the Church's Faith: Paul and his Recent Interpreters.* Grand Rapids. 1988. See also D. A. Carson. *Divine Sovereignty and Human Responsibility.* Atlanta, Ga. 1981. pp. 86-95
3. E. P. Sanders, *op. cit.* p.426
4. For some insight into the varied stances to be found today within Seventh-day Adventism, see M. Pearson. *Millenial Dreams and Moral Dilemmas.* New York. 1990, and *So Much in Common: Documents of Interest in the Conversations between the World Council of Churches and the Seventh-day Adventists.* Geneva. 1973

6

Respecting Scruples

Nobody can be saved by self-effort. Salvation is always God's gift; it is never our achievement.

Paul was utterly convinced of this. If this was so, then, it followed that there was no way people could be saved by keeping the Mosaic Law.

Does this mean then that he ignored the Law altogether and acted as if it did not exist? No! As we shall see later, he was aware that the Law given at Sinai was an important means of showing people what God is like. It is, of course, based on God's own character. He requires certain conduct from human beings because he is of a certain character himself.

This is a great help and challenge to us as Christians. It means that we can see from the Law what kind of qualities God looks for in his people.

Neither should we forget that Paul was a Jew, with a burning passion to see his fellow-Jews won to Christ. Simply to ignore the Law, which meant so much to them, would be deeply upsetting and would undoubtedly harm the cause of the gospel he loved so dearly.

Paul also wanted to see Jew and Gentile relating to each other constructively and happily as they took their places as Christians in the local churches. He was interested in harmony, for anything else was likely to compromise the witness of the gospel and disgrace the name of the Lord.

This was another good reason for taking the Jewish preoccupation with the Law seriously. To help people settle down
together you need to treat their differences realistically and
constructively and not brush them under the carpet.

What happened at Rome?

A study of Romans chapters 14 and 15 tells us a lot about
the Roman church and we can also learn important things
about Paul from it.

There was a large colony of Jews at Rome. We know that
some of them, as well as many Gentiles there, were converted to Christ.

At the time Paul wrote his letter to the Roman Church,
there were two parties, or at least two tendencies, in it. One
he calls 'weak' and the other 'strong'. It seems more than
likely that the 'weak' were mostly Jews and the 'strong'
mostly Gentiles.

It is worth noting though that at one point Paul, a Jew
himself, says, 'We who are strong ought to bear with the
failings of the weak and not to please ourselves' (Rom.
15:1). The way he phrases this makes it clear with which of
these two points of view he identified himself.

How did the two groups differ?

The 'weak' still observed the food laws of the Penta-
teuch, the Five Books of Moses. In fact some of them, to be
on the safe side in a Gentile environment, seem to have
abstained from meat-eating altogether (Rom. 14:2). They
also observed the special days of the Jewish calendar,
probably not only the Sabbath but also feast days and other
special occasions.

It is not surprising that many Jewish believers had this
outlook. In fact, in the story of Peter and Cornelius recorded

in Acts 10, we can see God using Peter's remaining scruples about the eating of 'unclean' meats in order to teach him a lesson about the acceptance of the Gentiles.

The 'strong' looked at things quite differently. They probably reasoned that, through Jesus, all the ritual laws were done away with. After all, had not Jesus declared all meats 'clean' (Mark 7:14-19)? Also, they would probably argue, all the feasts and other special days must have been abolished too.

Unfortunately, each of the groups tended to look down on the other. The 'weak' reckoned the 'strong' to be libertarians, without much conscience, while the 'strong' reckoned the 'weak' to be legalists who had not grasped the fact that Christ has set us free. There was pride and elitism in both attitudes.

Imagine you had been a leader in the early church. How would you have dealt with this situation?

The church at Rome consisted of a number of groups of believers meeting in various homes. We can see this from Romans 16. Here then surely was the key to a good practical solution! Suggest to them that they divide into two different churches! This would remove the problem at one stroke and everybody would be happy.

Everybody, that is, except Paul!

In fact, he handled the problem quite differently. What he did was to go back to the gospel itself and spell out some of its implications for the present situation. This was something they could in fact have done for themselves, but they were not seeing things clearly enough.

He says, 'Accept one another, then, just as Christ accepted you, in order to bring praise to God' (Rom. 15:7). If we have been reconciled to God, it follows that he has also reconciled us to each other. When I come to the foot of the cross, I meet others there and I find in them my brothers and sisters.

What upset Paul was the apparent failure of the two groups at Rome to accept one another wholeheartedly as brothers and sisters in Christ.

This shows how gospel-dominated he was. If God has accepted my fellow Christian then I must accept him too. I must not erect barriers to church fellowship when God has broken down all barriers at great cost through the death of his Son.

If the Roman Christians were to take the implications of the gospel seriously, this would mean that such matters would not divide them. Even if their practice continued to be somewhat diverse, there would be no breach of fellowship between them.

Was nobody to change, then? Yes! The 'strong' needed to learn not to ride rough-shod over the scruples of others, for this was not the way of that love and peace to which God has called us all.

So the members of the 'strong' group should consider their actions very seriously in the light of the reconciling work of Christ. They were of course free, but, as he wrote to the Galatians, in their freedom they should serve one another (Gal. 5:13). After all, in serving his Father Christ served us all, and it cost him his life.

What happened at Jerusalem?

If you read the Epistle to the Galatians and then go on to study the record of Paul's ministry in Acts you may find some of the incidents recorded in the latter difficult to understand. You may, in fact, be inclined to accuse Paul of inconsistency.

In Galatians he is most emphatic in declaring that the Christian is free from the Law. He accuses the false teachers there of preaching a false gospel.

Yet in Acts 18:18, Luke tells us that Paul had a vow. Luke's reference to Paul's hair being cut, presumably at the end of the period of the vow, clearly indicates what kind of vow it was. The Nazarite vow involved growing the hair and abstaining from alcohol for a period (Num. 6).

Was this inconsistency on Paul's part?

We are not told the reason for his vow, although Jews often used this way of showing their gratitude for some special blessing from God. In Acts 21, however, there is another incident which will help us to understand this one rather better.

On that occasion, James and the Jerusalem elders gave Paul a warm welcome when he arrived in their city. They were however worried about false reports which were circulating among the Jewish believers at Jerusalem. According to these rumours, he had abandoned the Law altogether, both for Jewish believers and also in his own personal practice.

To preserve his testimony among the Jewish believers therefore he was asked to link up with four men who had a vow. He was to make himself responsible for their expenses. This he did.

Does this reveal a failure of nerve on his part, something parallel to Peter's refusal at Antioch to eat with the Gentiles (Gal. 2:11ff)?

Not really. We can see his action simply as the product of his concern not to put a stumbling-block in anybody's way. The vow Luke tells us about in Acts 18 may have been motivated in the same way, or it may simply have been a personal expression of gratitude to God. Perhaps it was both.

What is worth noting though is that to fulfil a Nazarite vow would be a particularly clear way of showing his respect for the Law. This is because it would be seen in his personal appearance. For a time his hair would be much longer than usual.

What happened at Lystra?

Paul arrived at Lystra during the course of his Second Missionary Journey. There he heard excellent reports about a man called Timothy, whose mother was a Jewish Christian but who had a Greek father (Acts 16:1-3). Paul was eager to make him a member of his travelling evangelistic team.

Before doing this, however, 'he circumcised him because of the Jews who lived in that area, for they all knew that his father was a Greek.'

In many societies the status of a person, whether in the family or in the nation, depends more on that of the mother than of the father. The Jews reckoned anybody who had a Jewish mother to be a Jew, no matter who the father was. This is true among them to the present day.

Why then was Timothy still uncircumcised? Probably when he was a baby his father had refused to allow this to take place.

The Jews were likely to regard this as an unacceptable situation. This would trouble Paul, because he was most eager to spread the gospel among them. Anything that hindered that spread was to be avoided.

There was of course no suggestion whatever that this act was needed to make Timothy right with God. He was already accepted by God in Christ. It was purely to help rather than hinder the progress of the gospel among the Jews.

It is very helpful to contrast this with the incident Paul writes about in Galatians 2:3-5. Here he mentions Titus and the pressure some 'false brothers' had imposed on him to agree to his circumcision. Paul makes it clear that he resisted this with all his might and main.

Circumcision was itself a leading issue in the Galatian situation. It was much more important than matters such as diet and special days, the kind of things about which the Roman Christians were falling out. They were matters of lifestyle, but this was more serious, for it was about accept- ance with God.

A man who did not keep the food laws faithfully was a bad Jew, but a man who was uncircumcised was hardly a Jew at all.

It was therefore the rite which, above all else, enabled Gentiles to embrace Judaism and become Jews in all but birth. Paul was insistent at Galatia that the Gentiles did not have to convert to Judaism in order to become Christians. This was why he was so opposed to the desire of some of them to be circumcised.

Does this show inconsistency on Paul's part? Why circumcise Timothy and refuse to do the same with Titus?

In fact, Paul is being utterly consistent here, but it is a gospel consistency.

Titus, unlike Timothy, was a full Greek. To have circum- cised him would have given the impression that the Gentiles needed circumcision and Law-keeping for salvation.

In each case, it was the gospel that was at stake. In Timothy's case, it was its spread, in that of Titus it was its truth.

What happened in Galilee?

There have been many attempts to show that Paul's outlook on things was different from that of Jesus. In fact, as we have indicated earlier, some writers have maintained that Paul changed the Christian faith into something quite different from what Jesus intended. It is therefore well worth noting that Paul's action in circumcising Timothy was very much in line with the actions of our Lord.

Matthew 17:24-27 records a most interesting and revealing incident.

Jesus and his disciples arrived in Capernaum at the time the temple tax was being collected. What was this tax? It was not Roman but Jewish. It was prescribed in the Law of Moses (Exod. 30:11-16), and was for the upkeep of the temple at Jerusalem.

The collectors of this tax approached Peter and asked him if his Master paid it. The very question is interesting. It suggests that Jesus was suspected of a somewhat liberal attitude towards the Law, at least towards the ritual law.

Peter should have referred the matter to Jesus himself. Instead, however, in characteristically hasty fashion, he said 'Yes!' He had heard Jesus talking about going to Jerusalem and dying as a result of falling foul of the religious authorities. Perhaps Peter's reply was dictated by a feeling that he must try to keep his Master on the right side of these men.

Jesus challenges him, and yet, as the story proceeds, it becomes clear that the Master intended paying this tax. In terms of necessity, the correct answer was in the negative, while in terms of expediency, it was in the positive.

Jesus says that it is only God's servants and not his sons who need pay the tax, and, amazingly, he included Peter with himself in the family of God! The one had membership in that family by nature, the other by grace.

Despite this, Jesus said they would pay the tax so that no cause of stumbling would be put in the path of the collectors. These men could not have been expected to understand the considerations advanced to Peter by his Lord. Non-payment was likely to prevent them from taking the claims of Jesus at all seriously.

Notice then that the Saviour was as concerned about the spread of the gospel as his servant Paul was. In fact, his commitment to it was so deep that it took him to Calvary.

He came to preach the gospel. He came also that there might be a gospel to preach.

Here, as in so many other instances, we find Paul's teaching and practice to be completely in line with that of Jesus.

All things to everybody

Read 1 Corinthians 9, and you will discover the key to so much of Paul's practice in his evangelistic work among all kinds of people. Especially you will discover why he went about things in somewhat different ways.

The passage makes clear that he had a passionate desire to reach people with the good news of Jesus. It was this desire, stemming of course from the call of God to him, that underlay his differences of practice.

He says that to the Jew he became like a Jew to win the Jews and so also with the Gentiles. He became, he says, 'all things to all men so that by all possible means I might save some. I do all this for the sake of the gospel, that I may share in its blessings' (1 Cor. 9:22,23).

So then the gospel mattered supremely, but so also did

the scruples of other people if they prevented them from accepting Christ and God's message in him.

What about today's church?

The implications of this for local churches today are considerable. We all need to think through how it will affect our approach to evangelism in the area where God has put us.

Are there Jews in our community? Jesus is their Messiah, although most of them do not recognize him. It is important that we show them his love. Remember that Christendom has a very bad record as far as relations with the Jews are concerned, and that they are not always able to distinguish between Christendom and Christianity.

What about Moslems? They too have strong scruples about matters of food and drink.

Respect for the gospel is likely to be enhanced if Jewish or Moslem neighbours are invited into our homes, but not if they are insensitively offered the kind of food their religion forbids them to eat. We have been freed from such restrictions by the gospel of grace but should still be bound by the claims of Christ's love, as was Paul.

Then there are implications for our life within the Christian community. Often Christians tend to fall out over purely outward things or over matters of secondary importance. Many issues which have divided local churches could have been dealt with in a better way if there had been a more gracious attitude on the part of those concerned.

In recent times, there have been battles in local churches over Bible translations, over particular praise books, over styles of worship, and so on. Frequently the older members are on one side and the younger on the other.

We need of course to distinguish between scruples that

are based on important principles and traditions that have no real biblical foundation. For the members of a local church to try to do this together can itself be a helpful and illuminating exercise.

If there is mutual respect and love, everybody will seek a way forward that honours the Lord and that maintains true Christian unity.

7

Feeling the Agony

What kind of image of 'theology' do you have?

Many people, even Christians, seem to think of theology as a study far removed from real life. It deals with 'heavenly' things and has little to do with what happens on Planet Earth. It is purely 'religious,' belongs very definitely to Sunday rather than to Monday, to the minister's study and not to the home, the office, the shop floor.

This means of course that it is a passionless pursuit, unless of course it gets into the hands of the religious bigot. In such a case its hair-splitting distinctions may turn a man into a relentless persecutor of his fellow-men, even of his fellow-Christians.

For most folk though theology is a subject that could never engender much emotion.

How far removed this image of it is from what we find in Paul's epistles! To be thinking about God (which is what the theologian does) filled his heart with deep feeling.

The greatness of God made him worshipful, the holiness of God filled him with awe, the wisdom of God with amazement, the grace of God with gratitude, the judgement of God with concern for the lost. Theology for Paul engaged all his mental powers but it could never be purely cerebral.

It is important however to realize that Paul's theology never took its rise, never gained its sense of direction, from his feelings. Emotion was its effect, never its cause. It was grounded in God's revelation of himself.

We would do well to remember this ourselves. If our minds need to be instructed by the Lord before we can begin to think his thoughts after him, how much reliance can be put on our fickle feelings. They are capable of even less objectivity.

Certainly the Spirit of God gave Paul new understanding, as his mind pondered the gospel and its many-sided significance, but this was always done in the light of revelation already given. It was the meeting in his mind of the old truth, the Old Testament, and the new, the gospel, that was used by the Holy Spirit to produce Pauline theology.

There can be no doubt that Paul had major theological problems arising from his conversion to Christ. If Jesus, the crucified and risen Jesus, really was God's Messiah, his previous understanding of the Old Testament had been seriously deficient.

No doubt the gospel shed wonderful new light on old truths but there would be difficulties too. Remember also that before long he was at the cutting edge of the Christian mission. Further problems arose within the context of that missionary work, and some of these troubled his mind deeply.

A sad experience

A really big issue arose when he preached the gospel of Jesus to Jews.

Everywhere he went, his starting-point was the local synagogue.

Philippi might seem to have been an exception, because he began there at a place of prayer on the banks of a river outside the city (Acts 16:13-15). Luke tells us that those at prayer were women. In fact, this was really a substitute for a synagogue, because the establishment of an official synagogue required the presence of at least twelve male Jews in a local community.

In many places the response of the Jews was very disappointing. Most chapters of Luke's account of Paul's missionary journeys yield at least one example of small response or, more often, hostile reaction against the gospel on the part of the Jews in a particular town.

Paul's own comments confirm Luke's account. In writing to the Thessalonians, he is very strong in his language. 'You, brothers, became imitators of God's churches in Judea, which are in Christ Jesus: You suffered from your own countrymen the same things those churches suffered from the Jews, who killed the Lord Jesus and the prophets and also drove us out. They displease God and are hostile to all men in their effort to keep us from speaking to the Gentiles so that they may be saved. In this way they always heap up their sins to the limit. The wrath of God has come upon them at last' (1 Thess. 2:14-16).

Do these words seem harsh to you?

In the light of what he says elsewhere, especially in Romans chapters 9 to 11, we should not read them in that way, but hear in them a note of deep sadness. Paul was a realist and he faces real facts here, but we can be certain they gave him no pleasure. After all, the Jews were his own people.

A painful problem

For all of us, a big problem arises when two apparently irreconcilable facts collide in our minds. We have to work at the matter and try to find some way of bringing the two together and resolving their clash.

What were the two facts for Paul?

God's election of Israel, and Israel's rejection of God.

We see Paul wrestling with this issue in Romans chapters 9 to 11. He faces both facts and seeks to resolve them. Of course, he did not do this unaided, for he was writing under the inspiration of the Holy Spirit. The work of the Spirit did not however relieve him of the need for serious thought but instead operated effectively through these thought processes.

Paul had been reared as a Jew and as a Pharisee. From his youth, he would have known he was a member of the chosen people, those on whom God had set his love. He would have been taught the stories of the patriarchs and would know about the great promises God made to them. Particularly thrilling would be the account of how God rescued his people from the terrible bondage they experienced in Egypt, giving them the land of promise.

In course of time, he would learn too that God had not always been pleased with his people. They had often rebelled against him. They had even been deeply unfaithful to him by worshipping idols of wood and stone. Because of this, he had punished them and eventually had removed them from the land so that once more they were under the heel of foreigners, this time the Babylonians.

God never gave them up completely, however, and in his grace he had brought them back to the land, where they had enjoyed some periods of complete freedom.

Certainly this was no longer the case, as both in the Holy Land and in the lands of their Dispersion, they were under the yoke of the Romans. This would not however last for ever. It was God's promise that, when his purposes in history had been fully accomplished, the Messiah would come. Then Israel would enjoy God's blessing in the land of promise for ever. This was the great God-given hope of Israel.

Paul's conversion to Christ did not lessen one whit his conviction of the Divine authority of the Scriptures he had known from his youth, so that these promises still needed to be taken seriously. In fact, they took on glorious new meaning because he believed Jesus was the Messiah God had promised. [1]

It would have been natural to anticipate that the Messiah would be welcomed with open arms from the Jewish people. In the event, however, this did not happen. The religious leaders had led the way in rejecting him during his ministry. Their bad example was followed in synagogue after synagogue both in the Holy Land and among the Jews in other lands.

This was, of course, a continuation of the attitude of many Jews to God's word in Old Testament days, and Paul would know this. We need however to recognize that there was a quite special seriousness in the situation now.

This was due to the fact that Jesus the Messiah was not simply a great man of God. It was sinful to reject God's word through any channel, and yet there was a special solemnity attached to the rejection of the Christ, for he was God's only Son, the Saviour of Israel and of the world.

Paul knew, of course, that Jesus was to come again, but in his eschatology, his understanding of the last times, the Messianic age had already been inaugurated by his first coming and by the great saving acts of the cross and the resurrection.

He writes, 'For no matter how many promises God has

made, they are "Yes" in Christ. And so through him the "Amen" is spoken by us to the glory of God' and 'He anointed us, set his seal of ownership on us, and put his Spirit in our hearts as a deposit, guaranteeing what is to come' (2 Cor. 1:20-22).

He also knew full well that blessing through the second advent could only come to people who had placed their faith in the Christ of the cross and of the empty tomb. He is coming 'to be glorified in his holy people and to be marvelled at among all those who have believed,' but 'He will punish those who do not know God and do not obey the gospel of our Lord Jesus Christ' (2 Thess. 1:8-10).

How then could God's promises to Israel find fulfilment when they were rejecting the very Christ through whom alone they could be fulfilled? This problem forms the theological context of chapters 9 to 11 of Romans.

Paul did not view this problem in a purely detached way. It stirred his emotions deeply.

Almost everybody feels a deep sense of emotional involvement in his community, his family, his city, town or village, his nation. This deep feeling has always been very strong among the Jews.

In the closing verses of Romans 8, Paul writes about the great blessings Christians have through their relationship to Christ. Finally, he says (vv. 38,39), 'For I am convinced that neither death nor life, neither angels nor demons, neither the present nor the future, nor any powers, neither height nor depth, nor anything else in all creation, will be able to separate us from the love of God that is in Christ Jesus our Lord.'

Now comes chapter 9. There could not be a greater contrast in emotional tone. He says (vv. 1-4), 'I speak the truth in Christ - I am not lying, my conscience confirms it in the Holy Spirit - I have great sorrow and unceasing anguish in my heart. For I could wish that I myself were cursed and cut off from Christ for the sake of my brothers, those of my own race, the people of Israel.'

Nothing can separate us from God's love in Christ, yet 'I could wish that I myself were ... cut off from Christ.' Here is a self-forgetful love that expresses itself in deep agony. Here in fact is a measure of identification with Jesus the Christ, who endured punishment for the sins of others, crying out, 'My God, my God, why have you forsaken me?' (Matt. 27:46)

Do you ever feel like that about the salvation of other people? Face the implications of that searching question.

An election within the election

Paul's inspired solution to the problem was original and yet he makes it clear that there is plenty of support for it in the Old Testament.

In Romans 9:6,7, he says, 'It is not as though God's word had failed. For not all who are descended from Israel are Israel. Nor because they are his descendants are they all Abraham's children.'

He goes on to point out that the Divine line of promise was always a selective one. It passed from Abraham through Isaac and Jacob rather than through Ishmael and Esau, so that there was an election within the election.

If this was so, then God is following exactly the same principle if there is a selection within the nation of Israel that was descended from Jacob. His two uses of the name 'Israel' in the verses we have quoted distinguish of course between Jacob, who was given 'Israel' as his new name, and the nation that sprang from him.

This was certainly contrary to what Paul will have learned in his home, at the synagogue and from Gamaliel. The fact that he felt the need to argue for it helps to reinforce this fact.

In New Testament times, Jews believed that the righteousness of the fathers (the patriarchs) would be credited to their unworthy children. The general thrust of Pharisaic teaching was that a Jew, just because he was a Jew, would inherit God's salvation, although some very obvious reprobates, such as Jeroboam the son of Nebat, would be excluded.

If there is an election within an election, an Israel within Israel, how are the elect revealed? They can be recognized by their faith. Since Christ has now come, of course, faith becomes quite explicitly trust in him. This must be so, for the response always called for in the gospel is trust in Christ.

In fact, as Paul had already shown in Romans 4 and in Galatians 3 and 4, and as the writer to the Hebrews would show in chapter 11 of his letter, faith was always what God commanded people to give in response to his saving revelation.

This emphasis on faith comes into Paul's argument before Romans 9 ends and it is found all through chapter 10.

At the start of chapter 11 then, he makes it clear that God has not rejected his people. On the principle of an election within the election, God's purpose and word have not failed. In fact, he is himself living proof of that, as are many other Christian Jews. This in fact makes a link with the important Old Testament theme of the godly remnant.

The future of Israel

What about the future? Paul continues to assert that faith is the only way Jews can be saved. The whole point of his preaching to Jews was to secure this response of faith. In fact if unbelieving Jews give up their unbelief and put their trust in Christ, they can still find acceptance with God.

It would not have been surprising if he had gone no further than this. After all, he had faced the problem and dealt with it.

But Paul did go further. He was convinced that the story of the Jews was not yet over. His study of Scripture had made him realize that many of the promises were couched not in selective but in universal terms as far as Israel was concerned. In some way or other, the fulfilment must match up to this dimension of the promise. So a time would come when 'all Israel' would be saved (Romans 11:26). This was not simply a possibility but a fact. It was the purpose of God and was sure to come to pass.

Meantime the unbelief of so many of the Jews had led the Christian preachers to take the gospel outside the synagogues and to proclaim it to Gentiles. Many of the latter had come to accept Jesus for themselves. Of course, much of Paul's own ministry was to the Gentiles.

Eventually, however, there would be a national conversion of Israel. In this way, there would be complete fulfilment of God's word about them.

This would take place when the deliverer would himself turn godliness away from them, and when God would take away their sins (v.27). He is quoting from Isaiah 59 here, but there is no doubt whatever that by the deliverer he understood Jesus the Christ.

Just as the salvation of the Gentiles was a revelation of God's great mercy, so it would be when this salvation would come to Israel. Paul ends this important section of his letter by extolling the marvellous wisdom of God. It is important for us to notice that Paul interpreted not only the present situation, but also the ancient Scriptures and God's plan for the future, entirely in terms of the gospel. There is not the slightest suggestion that God's future provision for Israel would be at all different from that rich provision he had already made, for Jew and Gentile alike, in Christ.

Here we can see once again how gospel-centred Paul was. He interpreted even a theme as all-pervasive in the Old Testament as the future of Israel entirely in the light of the gospel of Christ.

The Gospel and the Jew today
What are the practical consequences of this for us today?

Without doubt our attitude to the Jews must be determined by the gospel, just as Paul's was.

It is sometimes said that there is an insuperable barrier to Jewish evangelism at the present time. This barrier has been built up over many centuries by the way Christendom has treated the Jews.

Now there can be no doubt that there is truth in this. Any Christian who has seriously tried to witness for Christ to Jews will certainly have discovered this.

Neither can we take refuge in the distinction between Christendom and Christianity. Real Christians have been involved at times in harsh treatment of the Jewish people.

Does it follow though that until the Christian Church as a whole has repented of this sin, there can be no real evangelism but only friendship and dialogue? This is being seriously said by some Christians today.

Be very clear as to the real consequences of this! It means adding one sin to another. The sin of harshness is serious, but do we show them love if we deny them the gospel of Christ, who alone is appointed by God as their Saviour? The answer surely is self-evident!

The gospel must be preached humbly to the Jews, it must be preached sensitively to them, it must indeed be accompanied by a spirit of penitence, but it must be preached.

References

1. For a study of Paul's attitude to the Old Testament, see E. E. Ellis, *Paul's Use of the Old Testament*. Edinburgh. 1957; also D. M. Smith. 'The Pauline literature' in D. A. Carson and H. G. M. Williamson (eds.). '*It is Written: Scripture citing Scripture*. Cambridge. 1988. pp. 265-291

8

Coping with Rejection

Paul was called by his Lord to preach the gospel and to plant churches. He found that these were by no means easy tasks.

In place after place, he encountered opposition, some of it fierce, and at times even potentially lethal. In the Acts of the Apostles, Luke often makes reference to this factor in the missionary life of Paul.

Sometimes Paul makes mention of such things in his letters. For instance, there is a moving passage in 2 Corinthians 11, where he writes about imprisonment, flogging and stoning as experiences that had come to him in the course of his gospel ministry.

There are also quite a number of passages where readers of Paul's epistles have detected that he is writing in answer to attacks made on the gospel or on him personally by opponents. Sometimes these opponents were non-Christians, while in other instances they were professing Christians.

One feature however occurs with almost monotonous regularity in Luke's account. We see there that Paul got a great deal of opposition from his fellow-Jews.

We have already noticed that this gave him some teasing theological and agonizing emotional problems. Remember though that he faced these problems almost every time he went into a synagogue and had the chance to speak and to declare the good news about Jesus the Christ. Clearly then it also presented him with practical problems.

What did he actually do in the face of such opposition. How did he handle it in practice?

In several ways:

He denounced it from Scripture

In Acts 28:14-31, Luke tells us what happened when Paul arrived in Rome.

We know from his letter to the Roman Christians that he had been longing to visit their great city for years, not, like some modern tourist, to see its great buildings, but to preach the gospel (Rom. 1:9-15; 15:23-24). At the time of writing, he was hoping to call on his way to Spain.

Now things had been taken out of his hands (although not out of the hands of his Lord) and he was arriving as a prisoner.

He was under house arrest but he still had a certain amount of liberty of action. We can be sure that he could not go into the local synagogue, as he had done so often elsewhere, but there were other ways of meeting his fellow-Jews. He called together their leaders and said he would like to speak to them about the hope of Israel.

As a result of this initial contact, a further meeting was arranged. This time a large number of Jews gathered and he preached Christ to them from the Old Testament prophets. The result, by now predictable, was division.

Paul then applied to them the words of God recorded in Isaiah 6:9,10, as follows:

'You shall indeed hear but never understand,
And you shall indeed see but never perceive.
For this people's heart has grown dull,
And their ears are heavy of hearing,

And their eyes they have closed;
lest they should perceive with their eyes,
And hear with their ears,
And understand with their hearts,
And turn to me to heal them.'

Incidentally, it is worth noting that each of the four Gospels quotes from this passage in Isaiah in reference to the failure of the Jews to receive God's message in Christ (Matt. 13:14,15; Mark 4:12; Luke 8:10; John 12:39,40). In the first three of these the words occur on the lips of Jesus himself. Here then is another example of Paul closely following his Lord.

In Romans 10, he again quotes from Isaiah when he is writing about the rejection of the gospel by Jews. In fact, there are no less than four quotations from that prophet in this one chapter.

In chapter 52:7, the prophet had eulogised the preaching of God's good news, which, in the next chapter (53:1) becomes the gospel of the atoning work of the Suffering Servant. That God should offer salvation through such a person seemed so incredible that, as Isaiah indicates, many would not believe it. Israel, the prophet says (65:2), was unbelieving and resistant to God's good word.

Not only does Paul quote Isaiah, but he also cites the words of Moses in Deuteronomy (Rom. 10:19), and Moses was of course the archetypal prophet of God.

Paul had found in experience that this rejection of God's word did not terminate when Old Testament prophecy came to its end. Many of the people of Israel were still rejecting it, as they had done before.

Now, of course, this rejection was particularly serious

because the gospel was the final message of God. It was for this Christ all the prophets had been waiting so eagerly, and yet when he came many of the people would not receive him.

Stephen had preached Christ before Paul's conversion. He too had seen Jewish opposition to the gospel to be a continuation of the attitude to God's message and messengers shown in the days of Joseph and of Moses (Acts 7).

So Stephen and Paul both saw the refusal of Christ and his gospel by their fellow-Jews not only as continuous with but also as the climax of a long and depressing history. Time and time again they had said 'No!' to God.

The one difference in their reaction to Stephen and Paul as Christ's messengers was that they killed Stephen while Paul survived to continue his service for his Lord.

He moved outside the synagogue to continue his preaching work.

Paul quite rightly began in the synagogue. For more than one reason, he preached the gospel 'to the Jew first' (Rom. 1:16).

In the synagogues he met Jews at worship, and of course they would be well versed in the Old Testament. There too proselytes and God-fearers, many of whom also would know the Old Testament well, could hear the message of Christ from his lips.

This meant then that, in biblical terms at least, the ground was prepared for the sowing of the gospel seed. The Old Testament is full of Christ for those who have eyes to see.

Not only so, but it was to the Jews that God had promised the Messiah. It was only right then that they should be the first to hear of Jesus, the fulfilment of these promises.

Add to all this the fact that Paul was himself a Jew, who loved his people, and whose great longing was to see them put their trust in Jesus as their Messiah, Saviour and Lord, and you will see that he could do no other than start in the synagogues.

Nevertheless it was the gospel that was all-important. If it was rejected in the synagogue it must be preached outside. We see this happening time and time again in the Acts of the Apostles.

Paul preached, for example, in the synagogue at Antioch-in-Pisidia (Acts 13:14-41). He warned his hearers against unbelief, and applied to them some strong words of Habakkuk (Hab. 1:5).

When many of them showed their opposition, he quoted from Isaiah 49:6: 'I have made you a light for the Gentiles, that you may bring salvation to the ends of the earth' (Acts 13:47). In these words, he had heard the Divine command to Christian preachers to proclaim the good news of Jesus beyond the bounds of Jewry.

Now this was just like showing a red rag to a bull. In New Testament times the Jews were deeply aware of their special position as the people of God.

They were prepared to see Gentiles coming to faith in the true God, the God of Israel, and being incorporated into Israel as proselytes. This did not challenge their special position. In fact, in some ways it reinforced it, for such Gentiles were really admitting the bankruptcy and untruth of their paganism and acknowledging the truth of what the Jews believed.

How different it was though if a preacher whose message had been rejected by the Jews turned to the Gentiles and began to preach it to them! This clearly implied that he considered pagans were more likely to be responsive than God's people themselves. This was deeply offensive.

Paul spoke to a large, antagonistic crowd from the steps of the Roman barracks in Jerusalem (Acts 21:40- 22:22).

Surprisingly, they listened quietly as he told them about his background. Even more amazingly, they let him recount the story of his conversion. Most surprising of all, they let him give an account of a subsequent vision he had of the risen Christ, when he warned him that the people of Jerusalem would not receive his testimony about his Master.

What was it then that provoked them to furious violence? It was when Paul declared, 'Then the Lord said to me, "Go, I will send you far away to the Gentiles." ' Luke then says, 'The crowd listened to Paul until he said this. Then they raised their voices and shouted, "Rid the earth of him! He's not fit to live!" '

In the synagogues of the Dispersion, it was the Pharisaic approach to Judaism that was standard. Paul also found, however, that unorthodox Jews were no more open to his message about Jesus as the Christ.

This too was a continuation of what had gone before. Old Testament prophets had not only found that many of the people and their leaders were unwilling to receive their message. They also met false prophets who contradicted that message.

This also happened to Paul. Luke tells us that in Cyprus the apostle met a Jewish sorcerer and false prophet (Acts 13: 6-12). The local Roman official was eager to hear the message of the gospel from Barnabas and Saul, but Elymas 'opposed them and tried to turn the proconsul from the faith'.

Where the Jews had stirred up the Gentiles also, he moved on to another place.

This happened, for instance, at Thessalonica and Berea (Acts 17:1-15).

At Thessalonica, Paul spent three Sabbath days proclaiming the gospel in the synagogue. Some Jews but more Gentiles believed. The unbelieving Jews were jealous of their success among the Gentiles and they stirred up trouble. The new Christians sent Paul and Silas away to Berea.

Luke writes very positively about the Berean Jews' initial response to the gospel. Then those who had been so antagonistic in Thessalonica got to know what was happening and stirred up trouble there too, presumably among the Gentile inhabitants of the city.

In each case, the new Christians in the locality were concerned to get Paul safely out of the city. This was probably because they had come to love him as a brother in the Lord and recognised that, as the leader of the preaching group, his life was likely to be at risk.

Why did Paul go along with this?

Was it because he was afraid of losing his life? Of course, nobody wants to die unnecessarily and it is not a Christian virtue to court an early death. There can be little doubt though that others would be in danger too, and it hardly fits Paul's character for him to move out of a dangerous situation to which his fellow-workers would remain exposed.

We should probably look therefore for an alternative explanation. One is not difficult to find. It seems very likely that it was chiefly Paul's great concern for the gospel that made him agree to move on.

The preaching of the gospel is always a matter of

urgency, but this was particularly true at this time. The number of messengers was small. If the gospel was to take root in the Graeco-Roman world, it was necessary to preach the message and establish churches in a good number of strategic centres just as soon as possible.

What though would Paul do today? After all, it is still the gospel that matters. If we get little or no response in one place, should we move to another?

In Britain and in many other countries, Christians are confronted not just by Jews but also by Moslems. The latter too have had some contact with the Biblical revelation, for Mohammed met both Jews and Christians. The Koran mentions quite a number of Biblical characters. Abraham, for instance, has a place of importance for Moslems as well as for Christians and Jews.

In many ways, Islam is farther away from Christianity than is Judaism, but in one respect it may seem nearer, for Moslems do find some place for Jesus. To them though he is not the Son of God nor did he die an atoning death for our sins. This means that in Christian witness to them error must be countered as well as truth declared.

In most places Jews and Moslems have made little response to the gospel, although there are exceptions. Should their comparative unresponsiveness make us leave them and move on?

Not necessarily. The situation now is somewhat different. The gospel has been planted in great centres virtually all over the world. There would seem to be room now for specialist ministries even in unpromising territory.

There are however still areas where the gospel has yet to be preached and others where gospel coverage is thin. We can learn from Paul's practice that adequate resources in people and money should be channelled into work in such places, and that this should be done as a matter of urgency.

If the preaching of the gospel is not urgent, what is?

When he could not move he continued to witness where he was.

Luke tells us in Acts 21 how Paul found himself in the hands of Jews who tried to kill him. The Romans took him into protective custody. He asked for permission to speak to the crowd. Then, as we have already seen, he began to proclaim Christ to them.

Later on he testified to the Sanhedrin, the great council of the Jews (Acts 23:1-10). Immediately after this, the risen Lord again appeared to him and told him that he would be bearing witness for him at Rome.

Before his arrival in Rome, he had many other chances of speaking of Christ, to Roman officials, to puppet rulers, to soldiers and seamen, and to many others.

All this time, his freedom of movement was restricted, but he could still witness to the gospel. Wherever he went the good news of Jesus was preached. He might be bound in chains, but, while he could speak, the gospel was as free as his voice.

In modern times, Christians in some Communist and Moslem lands have found themselves imprisoned or subject to locational restrictions. Like Paul, they have continued to witness in any way open to them, often at considerable cost to themselves.

Such brave believers ought to have the constant prayer support of those who enjoy greater freedom.

We too should be using our freedom to preach Christ, for our liberty to do so may not last for ever.

9

Dealing with Authorities

Christians may not be of the world but they are in it. This is an inescapable fact of life. We may not like it, but there is nothing we can do about it.

Because we are in the world, we find ourselves part of a structured society. We cannot do exactly as we like. Somebody is in authority. We may be free but there are limits to the exercise of that freedom, especially in our relations with other people.

This is true in most departments of life. A child discovers it early in life when he finds he cannot get out of his cot or crawl up the stairs because there is a barrier there. A girl leaving school finds that her employer does not take too kindly to late arrival at work. Even the secretary of the golf club is liable to get upset if I spend two hours trying to improve the way I tackle the fifth hole when there is a queue of other golfers behind me.

This is as it should be. The Bible recognizes the evil possibilities of a society in which nobody is in charge and everybody pleases himself as to what he does. It is after several chapters recording evil after evil that the Book of Judges closes with the words, 'In those days Israel had no king; everyone did as he saw fit' (Judges 21:25).

One of the Bible's most important passages on the function of human government is in one of Paul's epistles, in Romans 13:1-7. Here he exhorts his readers to obey the secular authorities God has set over them, to recognise their function in the punishment of evildoers and to pay taxes to them.

How did all this work out for Paul himself? What can we learn from his conduct in the world of yesterday for our conduct in the world of today?

There is no shortage of material. Luke has given us so much that it seems likely one of his reasons for writing Acts was to show that Christians were good citizens and that, in this respect, the Roman authorities had vindicated the servants of Christ many times over .

Things did not, however, start well.

Wrong treatment at Philippi (Acts 16:16-40)
This is the first encounter Paul had with secular authorities, at least it is the first recorded by Luke.

The small town of Philippi had an importance much greater than its size. It was a 'colony' of Rome, and, as such, had its own magistrates. The administration of the law there should have been first-class, but on this occasion it was not.

Paul and Silas were accused, among other things, of disturbing the peace. There is no suggestion in Luke's account that this charge had any foundation. It seems the magistrates simply acted on information supplied by antagonists of the gospel without checking on it. Yet Paul and Silas were given a severe public beating and had to spend the night in the town jail.

The authorities seem to have decided this was enough to teach them a salutary lesson. In the morning they gave instructions that they were to be released.

Paul protested at what had happened. He and Silas were Roman citizens and therefore had special rights. These had been flagrantly disregarded the previous night. They certainly should not have been beaten nor imprisoned without trial.

So we can see that Paul did not hesitate to make use of the status he had. It is true that what had been illegally done could not be undone, but he felt it was not right for the authorities to get away with misconduct.

Was something at stake for the gospel? He probably believed there was. It was important for it to be established that there was nothing offensive to the Roman law in the Christian faith nor in the endeavour to promote it more widely.

How does this apply today? If, for instance, a country has freedom of religion written into its constitution, it is surely right not to accept persecution by the authorities without reminding them of this.

Of course, we need to remember that sometimes these authorities may have such power that no protest, even on legal grounds, would have any effect and might well exacerbate the situation. In the days of the Communist regimes in eastern Europe, however, on several occasions protests made on behalf of Christians by people outside the country have eventually had the desired effect.

Trouble at Thessalonica and Berea (Acts 17:1-15)

We have already noticed that the gospel often got a bad reception from the Jews. In Thessalonica, the capital of Macedonia, they tried to get the local authorities to act against Paul and Silas. They did this by going into the market-place and inciting mob violence.

Paul and Silas were nowhere to be seen, so they dragged Jason, the leading local Christian, and his friends in front of the magistrates and accused them of harbouring trouble-makers. Roman officials were always concerned about law and order and were bound to take seriously a charge of disturbing the peace.

There was however a particular slant to the charge, which made it much more serious. 'They are all defying Caesar's decrees, saying that there is another king, one called Jesus' (Acts 17:7). A severe beating might be reckoned sufficient punishment for causing a riot, but sedition could carry the death penalty.

Can we learn anything from this? Jesus proclaimed the kingdom of God, but it has often been noticed that Paul rarely uses kingdom language in his epistles. This may have been quite deliberate to avoid just the sort of charge made at Thessalonica. Some official might have got hold of one of the letters and misunderstood it. [1]

There are many different ways of expounding the gospel. We cannot avoid causing offence by our preaching. By its very nature, the gospel cuts right across the normal thought-patterns of people.

Accepting this inevitability, however, and avoiding the temptation to trim our message to suit the likes and dislikes of people, it is important for us not to court misunderstanding by our language.

Suppose a preacher from a royalist country were to visit the USA or some other republic and to say, 'The Christian faith proclaims the authority of a King who is superior to a president.' He would have only himself to blame if he found himself accused of trying to foment anti-republican sentiments.

The city officials in Thessalonica took bail from the local Christians and released them. The strangers against whom the chief charges had been laid had disappeared. It is likely that, in the terms of the bail, Jason was to see to it that Paul and Silas did not return to the city.

On the messengers of the gospel went to Berea. This was a little off the beaten track, but it was quite a large city. A strong church established there would have plenty of evangelistic challenge and opportunity.

Luke was a Gentile, and his adverse comments on Jewish reaction to the gospel might make the reader think he was anti-Semitic. This would be a mistake. He writes very warmly about the Berean Jews and their eager reception of the Christian message.

Soon however Jews arrived from Thessalonica and trouble from a local mob started all over again. Once more the Christian preachers moved on.

There will be times when itinerant Christian preachers, facing persecution in one area and knowing that there is much need elsewhere, will move on, while at other times they will stay and face the persecution along with the local Christians. Circumstances alter cases, and missionaries and others facing such situations need the prayers of their Christian friends that right decisions may be made.

Preaching to the intellectuals (Acts 17:16-34)

The Acropolis in Athens, with its beautiful buildings, especially the magnificent Parthenon, was a sight many a traveller would cover many miles to see. This is still true for tourists in the eastern Mediterranean.

Paul was no tourist. As a highly cultured man, he probably lacked nothing in aesthetic appreciation, but he was in Athens on much more serious business, the proclamation of salvation through Christ.

Beautiful as these buildings were, they had been erected to foster pagan worship. The Parthenon housed a great statue of Athena, the local goddess.

In the course of his preaching in the market-place, Paul met a number of philosophers. The Epicureans and Stoics would spend many a day disputing with each other. Now they had somebody else to argue with.

Athens had been the most important philosophical centre in the Greek world for centuries, and the Athenians enjoyed listening to good communicators, especially if they were disputing with each other. Athens was no longer a free city, however, and it is not surprising that the Romans, who liked local affairs to be neat and tidy, appear to have given power to the ancient court of the Areopagus to regulate this sort of thing.

With pagan religion visible on the hill of the Acropolis, with the busy market-place near the site of the court crammed with people, and with the philosophers and the city authorities sitting before him in the most ancient court in Athens, Paul began to declare the truth of the gospel.

It was a fine opportunity.

He immediately sought to grip their attention and relate his gospel to the local situation by his reference to the altar to an unknown God.

A careful study of his sermon shows that it was closely related to the interests both of the Epicureans and the Stoics and yet challenged the outlook of both. [2]

Moreover Athenian pride in the tradition that their ancestors sprang fully-grown from the soil of Attica would have taken a knock by his Bible-based assertion, 'From one man he made every nation of men' (Acts 17:26). All this led up to the proclamation of Jesus as risen from the dead and destined to be the Judge of all.

A Christian preacher may get an unexpected opportunity of proclaiming the Christian message in some non-Christian environment. If there are no strings attached, this is to be seized with both hands and prayerfully used in the interests of the gospel.

It perhaps goes without saying, however, that he will need to find out something about the outlook of those who have invited him, so that they can quickly see the relevance of the gospel to them. Paul was straight and clear in his preaching, but without discourtesy. Faithfulness and sensitivity are not enemies but friends.

Was he given permission to continue his preaching?

Luke tells us, 'When they heard about the resurrection of the dead, some of them sneered, but others said, "We want to hear you again on this subject." At that, Paul left the Council. A few men became followers of Paul and believed. Among them was Dionysius, a member of the Areopagus, also a woman called Damaris, and a number of others. After this, Paul left Athens and went to Corinth' (Acts 17:32-18:1).

It looks then as if judgement on permission to preach unhindered was suspended meantime, but that Paul did not wait in the city. Possibly he concluded that there were enough converts to constitute a church and that he should himself move on. Maybe he would have had to remain silent until such time as the court convened again. The preaching of the gospel was too urgent at that time to permit delay and so he proceeded to Corinth.

The content of the gospel judged not to be contrary to Roman law (Acts 18:12-17)

What happened at Corinth, the capital city of Achaia, was of great importance for the status of the gospel in the Roman Empire at this time.

Here Paul again fell foul of the Jews who this time brought him to court themselves. They accused him of promoting an illegal religion.

Probably this accusation started life among them as the contention that the gospel was against God's law. Somebody may then have suggested that there could be a case against Paul in the secular courts. Judaism was a permitted religion, but was what Paul was preaching really authentic Judaism? They did not think so, and they hoped to persuade the authorities that what Paul was proclaiming put him outside the law.

This proved a very unwise move on their part.

Paul, possibly to his disappointment, did not have to speak at all in his defence. As soon as the governor heard the nature of the issue, he ruled that there was no charge to answer and dismissed the case. He could not be expected to understand or rule on the finer points of religious disputes.

This ruling was almost certain to have had wider repercussions. Gallio, the proconsul, was an eminent man, the brother of the great Seneca, and renowned for his moderation, wit and wisdom.

There is little doubt that Luke saw the hand of God in this. Such a lot could have been written about Paul's work at Corinth but he uses precious space to record this incident. Gallio's ruling may well have been God's way of protecting Christianity from the charge of illegality during the crucial years of its initial spread in the Roman Empire.

In 1965, an unsuccessful attempt to overthrow the government of Indonesia led to the passing of a new law. Everybody was to have a religion and this was to be recorded on his or her papers. As a result many Communists who had been Moslems but had experienced resistance to their attempted return to Islam began to attend Christian churches. Many were converted.

God still uses political decisions in the interests of the gospel.

Antagonism from commercial interests (Acts 19:23-41)
The impact of the gospel, through the ministry of Paul, had already been felt financially. At Philippi, there was a slave-girl who worked as a fortune-teller. Paul had been used to expel an evil spirit from her. Her owners were furious because they could no longer make money by exploiting her. This sparked off the trouble that led to the imprisonment of Paul and Silas (Acts 16:12-40).

In Ephesus there was a huge temple to Artemis. It was reckoned one of the seven wonders of the world. The idol-makers began to feel the effects of Paul's gospel ministry there and to be afraid that their business would suffer.

Two of Paul's preaching team found themselves in the midst of a mob, which rushed them into the theatre, where general assemblies of the citizens were normally held.

It is interesting to note that Luke tells us that some of the provincial officials were friends of Paul and that they strongly advised him not to venture into the theatre. It looks then as if the gospel had penetrated the ruling classes, perhaps aided by Gallio's earlier ruling. Corinth and Ephesus were both major seaports and news of this could have been conveyed swiftly from the one to the other.

The town-clerk took charge of things. He was not a Roman but the highest local Ephesian official. The Romans would hold him responsible if things got out of hand.

Just as Gallio had done, this man recognized that the Christian preachers had done nothing indictable. They had not abused the local religion either physically or verbally. Nothing could be settled by such an unruly meeting anyway, and, if there were legitimate complaints, they must be settled properly through the courts.

At first this is a little puzzling. If Paul had been saying that idols were not deities at all, how can this be squared with the town clerk's statement that the Christian preachers did not blaspheme the goddess?

It is probable that the preaching had consisted mostly of positive declaration of the gospel with the attack on idolatry as a comparatively minor element in it, and couched in general terms rather than as an onslaught on the worship of the local goddess.

Positive preaching of the gospel is normally the most effective way of demolishing idolatry and error. Proclaim the truth and, through the witness of the Spirit, it will have power to overthrow the strongholds of Satan.

Under Roman Protection (Acts 21:27-24:27)

In Jerusalem Paul was rescued from the wrath of a Jewish crowd by the order of an officer of the Roman garrison there. He proposed to have him flogged prior to interrogating him. Paul objected to this on the grounds that he was a Roman citizen and had not been found guilty, and his objection was heeded.

He was kept under protective custody both in Jerusalem and in Caesarea, the Roman administrative centre of the country. The Roman authorities were determined that he should not get into the hands of the Jews when there was no proper charge in Roman law against him.

His enemies tried to get him condemned but always these attempts failed. When a plot against his life came to light, the commander of the Jerusalem garrison provided a large military escort to make certain he would get to Caesarea with speed and in complete safety.

This is impressive evidence not only of the fact that God uses non-Christian rulers and their servants to accomplish his ends, but also that he may do so in a quite exceptional way. For instance, in a former Communist country, magnificent educational facilities created for teaching Communism and that were lying empty were put at the disposal of evangelical Christians when they had arranged a course for the training of pastors!

We can be thankful for places where the authorities are protective of the rights of Christians to gather for worship and to preach the gospel, and we should always be concerned for Christians living in places where these things are lacking.

Paul was concerned that the churches should pray 'for kings and all those in authority, that we may live peaceful and quiet lives in all godliness and holiness. This is good, and pleases God our Saviour, who wants all men to be saved and to come to a knowledge of the truth' (1 Tim. 2: 1-4).

This strongly suggests that the desire for peace and quiet was not viewed simply as a desirable end in itself, but as a means to the spread of the gospel.

The appeal to Caesar (Acts 25-28)

Paul profited from being in protective custody. Eventually he discerned that he might well be put into the hands of the

Jews and so he appealed to Caesar.

As Roman law stood at that time, a Roman citizen might make this appeal if he was in danger from violence or if the charges against him were sufficiently serious. In Paul's case, the authorities apparently had no option but to send him to Rome.

What his motives were here it is not possible to tell with certainty. He wanted of course to preserve his life and to be able to continue his evangelistic work. He would know too that this would be a way of getting to the capital of the empire. As we have seen, his letter to the Romans, written some years earlier, makes it clear that he was eager to get to Rome, to preach the gospel there.

This makes us realise that a Christian can make use of the law and any rights or privileges it confers on him if to do so would advance the gospel. There are times when God works in history or in the lives of his people in a way that is quite independent of any action on their part. There are also times when we have to take definite steps ourselves.

There can be little doubt though that Paul will have prayed much about this situation and about what he should do.

After many adventures and much evidence of God's protecting hand on his life, Paul finally arrived in Rome. For two years he was there, under house arrest but, as Luke makes clear in the closing verses of Acts, quite free to preach the gospel to all who came to see him.

Five of Paul's letters, those to the Ephesians, Philippians, Colossians and Philemon and the Second Epistle to Timothy, were written from prison. We will not just now trace the story of his two imprisonments in Rome (for he appears to have been released for a while), but simply remark that in these letters some of the profoundest doctrine and some of the most challenging ethics in the New Testament are to be found.

So, in Roman custody, he was not only able to preach the gospel but also to teach and apply its deeper truths to those already in Christ.

No doubt at times he will have been very concerned about his situation, for he was human, but God was at work in it all for the glory of his name and for the spread of the glorious gospel of Jesus.

References

1. Paul's occasional use of kingdom language is of such a character as to indicate its spiritual nature. George Johnston comments, for instance, on 1 Corinthians 6:9,10, 'He is using the old Kingdom idiom, but clearly not with reference to an earthly monarchy and so not to any dominion that might rival the Roman Empire.' '"Kingdom of God" sayings in Paul's Letters' in P. Richardson and J. C. Hurd (eds.). *From Jesus to Paul: Studies in Honour of Francis Wright Beare*. Waterloo, Ontario. 1984

2. See B. Gürtner. *The Areopagus Speech and Natural Revelation*. Translated by C. H. King. Lund. 1955.

10

Confronting Paganism

Sometimes in studying the Scriptures it can provoke thought for us to ask ourselves what we might expect to find in them which is not there. There are good reasons for this kind of thing and it is worthwhile giving such matters some thought.

For instance, why is there so little in the Acts of the Apostles about the clash between the gospel and paganism?

After all, this was a leading feature of the modern missionary movement for many years. In many places it is still true of it today, and we might expect it to have been an even more prominent feature at this early stage of church history.

There is however a special reason for this.

Paul and his friends normally started in the synagogues. If their preaching there resulted in the formation of a church, they would soon move on. It would then be at the next stage that evangelism would take place among the pagan peoples of the area. This would be an enterprise of the infant local church rather than of the apostolic group.

Why did they operate in this way?

God had been preparing the Jews for the coming of Christ. The Old Testament is the inspired record of that preparation, and it was read at every synagogue service.

It is full, for instance, of prophecies fulfilled in Jesus the Christ. These are many-sided, for the significance of his person and work is also many-sided.

Also there are many examples there of God's power to rescue his people from danger. There was the Exodus from Egypt, there were many deliverances from invading armies during the time of the Judges, Jonah's rescue from the water and from the great fish, and many others. These anticipate the great Rescue from Satan and sin that God effected through the cross of Christ..

In addition, people were prepared by the fact that they could have fellowship with God through the sacrificial system, which also taught them many great lessons about God, about sin and atonement. These sacrifices were really provisional means of fellowship with God until Christ came. Just as banknotes are symbolic and at one time used to represent actual gold in the national bank, so the Old Testament sacrifices were symbols of the one true Sacrifice, which Christ was to make at the cross.

Because of the dispersion of the Jews, there were synagogues in many cities and towns all over the Graeco-Roman world. In them the Scriptures were read and worship was offered to the true and living God.

These centres of worship and preaching proved attractive to many Gentiles. They were able there to become acquainted with the Old Testament preparation for the gospel of Christ.

Could these Gentiles of the synagogue be called 'pagan' any more? In a great many cases, this would have been quite inappropriate.

At first, we might be inclined to make a firm distinction between proselytes and God-fearers. The Jews made a very distinct difference between these two groups.

The former were Gentiles who had been through the formalities of transfer from paganism to Judaism, whereas the latter, although interested in the Jewish religion, had not. There can be little doubt, however, that many of the God-fearers had already come to faith in the true God, but had not yet taken the final formal steps.

These Gentiles were not only a fruitful field for evangelism but also potential evangelists themselves. They lived in the Gentile community and they were familiar with its social and religious culture. Just as today, missionary leaders consider national Christians to be more effective evangelists than missionaries from another culture, so it must have been then.

There are however a few recorded examples of evangelism outside the synagogues among pagan peoples, and we will look at some of them.

Polytheistic Paganism

In Acts 14:8-20, Luke tells us what happened at Lystra.

There was apparently no synagogue preaching there. Perhaps there were not enough Jews there to form a synagogue.

This city had a certain prestige as a Roman 'colony', and so it was able to govern its own affairs, but most of the population were simple people with a tribal background. Hellenism had taught them new names for old gods, and they were familiar with the main gods of the Greek pantheon.

Ovid, the Roman writer, records an interesting and illuminating legend [1]. The gods, Zeus and Hermes, disguised as ordinary mortals, had paid a visit to this general area. Nobody would give them a bed for the night except one poor couple who welcomed them with a generosity they could ill afford. As a result the other houses were destroyed but theirs was transformed into a temple.

A miracle was performed by God in connection with the ministry of Paul and Barnabas. Perhaps remembering the legend, the crowds concluded that Zeus and Hermes had returned. There was an attempt to worship them.

Was this opposition to the gospel? On the face of it, it may not have seemed so, but in reality it was, for the gospel is in fact God's instrument for stamping out paganism and its accompanying idolatry.

Paul and Barnabas were horrified at what happened and they reacted with an immediate and vigorous protest.

They then began to preach to the people. Some readers have been puzzled by the absence of any reference to Christ here, but we need to remember that Luke's account of the history of the church had to be highly selective. He probably took the Christian content of the preaching for granted, but concentrated on its distinctive feature on this occasion.

This feature was the proclamation of the God of creation and providence.

Unlike the Jews, these people had not had any historical or literary preparation for the gospel. God had however shown them his beneficence by the provision of food.

There is little doubt that then Paul and Barnabas will have gone on to speak of the crowning act of God's goodness to them in the coming of Christ. In him there was the one true visitation of God in human form and he had given himself for the salvation of sinners.

Jews from Antioch and Iconium arrived and provoked the crowd to physical violence against the preachers. Paul and Barnabas then moved on to another place to continue their preaching.

We see here then that Paul and his friends reacted to

pagan opposition in the same way as they did when they were opposed by the Jews.

At this stage of things, it was important to spread the gospel as widely and as quickly as possible. Why keep trying to implant seed in extremely hard ground when there might well be better soil further on?

Today, as we have earlier suggested, the situation is different. There is still great need of evangelism, even of a pioneering type, for there are still many millions of un-reached people. There are however churches in most of the world's countries and these are actual or at least potential centres for the spread of the gospel in their areas.

In many places, missionary church planters are still urgently needed, but the Christian church ought to be able to provide personnel both for these and also for workers in hard areas. There is here a challenge both to active mission-ary service and to prayer.

We have already seen that the disturbance in Ephesus, recorded in Acts 19, was motivated more by economics than religion, and so we will move on to the visit to Malta recorded in Acts 28:1-10.

Near this island, the ship on which Paul was being taken as a prisoner to Rome was wrecked. He and the rest of the passengers and crew, already drenched with sea water, arrived on the island in wet, cold weather. Luke, who seems to have been in the party, wrote of the 'unusual kindness' of the local people.

Paul was attacked by a snake. This immediately made the islanders think he was a malefactor and that justice would not allow him to escape, despite his rescue from a watery grave. It is unlikely this is a reference to justice in the abstract but rather to the Greek goddess Dike. Her name, meaning 'Justice,' is the actual word Luke uses here.

When Paul suffered no harm, they concluded he was a god.

His reaction to this is not recorded, but there can be no doubt at all he would have rejected it as decisively as he had done at Lystra. This may be another example of the fact that once Luke had established a certain principle by recording an event, he saw no need to go into full detail on a subsequent occasion. His main concern in this section of his narrative seems to have been with the providence of God seen in so many ways on Paul's journey from Caesarea to Rome and he does not tell us whether or not a church was established on Malta.

This and the incident at Lystra show that, despite what Gilbert Murray called the 'failure of nerve' in the religious scene in the Graeco- Roman world at this period[2], paganism still played an important part in the thinking of ordinary people.

As events turned out, the gospel of Jesus Christ proved far more powerful than any of the old faiths. Its triumphant march against paganism continued well beyond New Testament times. Indeed, it continues today. It is still the pure gospel preached in the power of the Holy Spirit (with or without signs and wonders performed at God's discretion) that is effective to overturn idols.

Occultistic Paganism

Occultism, whether ancient or modern, is essentially pagan. There are today some so-called 'churches' which call themselves 'Christian spiritualists'. They try to put people into contact with the dead through mediums at the same time as professing to follow Jesus Christ. This is really simply pagan occultism masquerading in Christian dress.

At Philippi, Paul and his friends met a female fortune-teller who had an evil spirit (Acts 16:16ff). Paul expelled the spirit by the power of the Spirit of God. The opposition then moved on to another plane, for the commercial interests of the owners of the girl were affected.

There has been a major resurgence of occultism in the West in recent decades. It has become part of the thinking of large numbers of people. Many who would never think of entering a church or turning to God in Christ to direct their lives, eagerly read the horoscopes in newspapers and magazines and look at their presentation on the television. In fact, for many people this is now an essential part of their daily routine.

Mere condemnation of this by Christians is not enough. The phenomenon may be sinister, but it also gives us a gospel opportunity.

God promises to guide the lives of his people. Not only so, but there is a special providence from him active in their lives. Perhaps there should be more emphasis on this dimension of the gospel today than there has been at times in the past.

Does preaching need to be accompanied by exorcism? At times, this may be necessary.

God has provided us, in Christ and through the Holy Spirit, with every spiritual resource needed in the battle with supernatural forces. Paul himself makes this clear in a great passage in Ephesians 6:10-20.

The spiritual armour plus the offensive weapons of the word of God and prayer, have all been provided by God. Trusting in Christ and filled with the Holy Spirit we may be confident in his power and victory.

The whole issue however raises important questions. What is the relationship between the spiritual, the psychical and the physical? How can we be sure whether certain phenomena belong to the domain of the Christian worker or to that of the psychiatrist? Is it wise for a Christian worker to move into this field without any experience and with little knowledge?

In general, it needs to be said clearly and plainly that a Christian confronted by what appears to be possession by an evil spirit should, when at all possible, seek advice and support from mature Christian workers.

Philosophical Paganism
Does the combination of these two words, the adjective and the noun, seem out of place? In fact it is not, as we can see from Acts 17:16-33.

This is a passage of great interest from several points of view, but not least because of the close relationship between paganism and philosophy that we find in the Athenian scene as presented here.

Paul did preach in the synagogue, but Luke particularly features his proclamation of the message in the market-place and before the court of the Areopagus.

We may infer from the account that a large crowd gathered in the market-place to hear what Paul had to say. He was preaching the good news of Jesus and featuring the resurrection. The Greek for 'resurrection' is feminine in form, and it seems that some, perhaps simply hearing snatches of the message from the back of the crowd, concluded that he was pressing the worship claims of two deities, the male being Jesus and the female Anastasis ('Resurrection').

A little later, although addressing at the court of the Areopagus a sophisticated audience including philosophers, Paul felt it appropriate to start from a particular phenomenon of Athenian paganism, the altar to an unknown god. The truth of the matter is that neither the Epicureans nor the Stoics had cut completely adrift from the prevalent paganism.

The Epicureans still believed in the existence of the Greek gods, although they said that their present interest in mortals was virtually nil.

The Stoics were pantheists, identifying God as the inner 'Soul' of the world, but this is of course was far from the Biblical revelation of God as the Creator and Ruler of all things. In various cultures, pantheism and polytheism have gone hand-in-hand as the religions of intellectuals and less sophisticated people respectively.

In some ways, the Epicureans and Stoics held opposite points of view. The Epicureans believed the gods created the world, but now had little interest in it. The Stoics believed that God and the world were alike eternal, but that God indwelt all things.

In his sermon, Paul both makes contact with and criticizes each.

He asserts the creation of the world by the one true God, but also the fact of his presence within his universe. He even quotes from pagan philosophers, although of course these extracts from Epimenides (Acts 17:28a) and from Cleanthes or Aratus (Acts 17:28b) by no means authenticate all these men had said but only the truth of these particular extracts.

Despite the fact that Paul is addressing people with no knowledge of the Old Testament, his message never loses contact with its biblical roots. In fact, the sermon is saturated with Old Testament language. Adam and Christ appear in the message (Acts 17:26,31), but they are not named. The names would mean nothing to the hearers, and what mattered of course was not their names but the significance of what they had done.

Paul found it expedient then to show that even the poets of the Greeks at times used language consonant with the message he brought.

This certainly did not mean that Paul's hearers could simply combine Christianity with their present philosophical or religious viewpoints. Paul knew full well that nothing short of a complete reorientation of their life and thought was needed and so he called on them to repent.

This meant of course that they must accept the risen Christ and that their life was to be lived in the light of his return to judge the world. They must therefore begin in a totally fresh way to learn of God through him.

Resurrection itself raised philosophical problems for them, although Luke indicates to us that there were a number of conversions.

This means then that, although Paul found in their own outlook some entrance points for the gospel, he did not in any way compromise its message.

To be real, conversion must be radical. We dare not give people the impression that Christ can simply fill an empty space in a life already full. He is not useful to fill life's small (or large) vacuums, for he will not be a Divine means to a human end. Rather he rightly demands to be the Lord of every part of life.

Non-Christian philosophy, just as much as polytheism or the occult, has on it the smell of death. Only the risen Christ can give life.

Those called to work among the pagans who worship idols, or the pagans who follow the horoscopes or tarot cards, or the intellectual pagans who follow the latest philosophy, will do well to become equipped with some knowledge but also to rely on the power of the risen Christ who alone can meet the needs of every kind of pagan.

Compromise with paganism within the church

Because conversion is to be radical, there can be no question of a Christian participating in pagan ceremonies. Paul makes this abundantly clear in 1 Corinthians 10:14-22.

He does not condemn eating in the home of an unbeliever (1 Cor. 10:27). This could of course be a good opportunity of witness for Christ. If though the meal is part of a religious ceremony in a pagan temple, that is another matter altogether.

Certainly there is only one God, so that the beings pagans worship are not real gods. Paul makes it clear however that the worship is in fact received, for there are demonic forces involved in the whole business. Demons are the recipients of the worship, and it is therefore unthinkable that a Christian should be involved in it.

Christians in some religious cultures may be particularly open to this kind of temptation.

Hinduism is so eclectic that it would probably be willing to swallow Christianity up completely, and so it is particularly important there should be no compromise with it. Christ will not be part of a system. He is only prepared to be Lord of all.

African indigenous religion still has power to attract and it is important for the Christian in that environment to be aware of the distinctiveness of the Christian faith. There have been a number of unhappy experiments in which elements of African religion have found their way into the outlook of Christians.

Until recently, Christians of the West might have seemed almost immune to this danger, but this is certainly not true now. There is a good deal of paganism in the different types of New Age thinking.

Here as elsewhere everything must be tested by Scripture. It was our Saviour who quoted the words, 'Worship the Lord your God, and serve him only' (Matt. 4:10: cf. Deut. 6:13ff.).

References

1. Ovid. *Metamorphoses* 8.626-724, mentioned in R. N. Longenecker. 'The Acts of the Apostles' in F. E. Gaebelein (ed.). *The Expositor's Bible Commentary*. Vol.9. Grand Rapids. 1981. p.435
2. Gilbert Murray, *Five Stages of Greek Religion*. Oxford. 1925. pp. 153- 207.

11

Defending his Apostleship

I have a book in my library that shows, from the way its pages fall when I open it, that I have read the first hundred pages or so several times. It is equally obvious that I have spent little time on the remainder of the book.

Why is this? For a perfectly good reason. The book was written about a hundred years ago. The first hundred pages or so deal in masterly fashion with an issue that will never grow old as long as the Christian church exists. The remainder deals with debates over issues that have changed their shape greatly since the book was written.

The scholarship is equally good throughout the whole book, but parts of it are no longer relevant and so it is not worth spending much time on these.

Eighty-eight chapters of our New Testament claim to be the work of the apostle Paul. These are filled with truth that is instructive, encouraging and challenging.

Six of these chapters, however, pose a puzzle for some modern readers. Why, with so much glorious positive truth to teach us, does Paul devote so much space to a defence of his apostleship? Did this really matter?

Even if it mattered then, does it matter now? Should we not just ignore these chapters in which he seems to be fighting some opponents over issues that are of no possible concern to us today?

This would be a great mistake.

Its crucial importance
The defence of status is usually unattractive.

Sometimes it is the product of deep personal insecurity. I do not really feel up to the job. I am almost convinced I am going to be a failure. I am pretty sure others are feeling this way about me too.

So, to cover up this insecurity and to convince both myself and them of my abilities, I lay great stress on my appointment to the work. The unspoken assumption is that the people who appointed me believed in me and so I must be equal to the task. Because of this I make an energetic defence of my status.

At other times it is the result of arrogance. I have a power complex. I am proud of my status and insist that others recognise me for what that status proclaims me to be - a cut above them. The psychologists may suggest that this too ultimately stems from insecurity.

There can however be a third reason. If my work is for the general good, if its validity depends on my status, and if that status is under attack, then my defence of it is absolutely right. In fact, in these circumstances, simply to give in without a fight would be cowardly and would show I cared more about peace than about the good of other people.

Paul's defence of his apostleship belongs to the third category. In fact it was not simply a matter of the public good, but also of the glory of God. Of course he had to put up a fight!

In fact, it may not be too much to say that the very future of Christianity as a world faith depended on it. Certainly, if Paul had given in, God in his sovereignty may have accomplished the same end through different means, but in actual fact we know that Paul was God's instrument for the fulfilment of an important purpose.

As we have seen, Paul saw with crystal clarity what the good news of Jesus meant for Gentiles. It was quite wrong for anybody to try to squeeze them into the kind of legalistic mould prescribed by Pharisaic Judaism. This would give the impression that God's way of accepting them was based, at least in part, on their merit.

Whenever the utterly gracious basis of the gospel was challenged, he contended for it vigorously. How important it was for him to do this!

If the early church had lacked somebody with such a vigorous commitment to free salvation, it could easily have become a mere sect of Judaism. There would still have been arguments about the Messianic claims of Jesus but even that issue would lose some of its importance, and the Christians would probably have lost the argument altogether eventually.

After all, if the cross was not God's full provision for our salvation, then what was it? If we have to add something to it, perhaps the Christ who died there was not really the Son of God at all? Perhaps, in fact, he was not the Messiah? In fact, some might have gone on to argue, perhaps he was actually an imposter?

What has this to do with the apostleship of Paul? A very great deal.

If he was not an apostle, then the authority of his teaching is open to question. Jesus appointed men to preach and teach his gospel and to establish the Christian church on a foundation of truth. Deny the apostleship of Paul and the basis of his teaching in the authority of Jesus himself is undermined. Can we really envisage what the New Testament would be like if we did not have any of his letters?

If apostleship carried no authority with it, two chapters in Galatians and four in 2 Corinthians need never have been written. If however Paul's preaching and teaching in Galatia and Corinth (and, of course, everywhere else) had the seal of the authority of the risen Christ upon it, then to fight against that preaching and teaching was to fight against Christ himself.

The issue at Galatia

This is quite clear in the Galatian epistle. It is in the first two chapters that Paul defends his apostolic status.

In chapters 3 and 4, as we have seen, he argues *theologically*. He agrees with the false teachers that the Gentiles need to become children of Abraham if they are to inherit God's promises. It is not however circumcision but faith that makes them his children. In chapters 5 and 6, he argues *ethically*. Certainly God cares about the quality of a Christian's life. High standards are not however secured by legalism but by dependence on the Holy Spirit as he makes our lives channels of the love of God.

These four chapters are very valuable, but they really depend on the first two. If Paul had not been an apostle, his reasoning in these chapters could be no more than the passionate expression of personal opinion. But if he was an apostle, these chapters immediately become the word of the living Christ.

He asserts his apostleship in the opening salutation of the epistle.

He begins his actual defence of it by focusing on the gospel. It immediately becomes clear that apostleship matters so much simply because the gospel matters so much. In fact, the value of apostleship, great as it is, is simply instrumental, a means to an end and not an end in itself.

This appears most clearly when Paul says, 'But even if we or an angel from heaven should preach a gospel other than the one we preached to you, let him be eternally condemned' (Gal. 1:8)! Paul included himself in a general anathema on the unlikely supposition that he would turn from the true gospel to proclaim some other. So then it is not Paul that matters, but the gospel.

These words of Paul are not the product of personal uncertainty nor of pride. They show as clearly as can be that Paul is not writing out of insecurity or arrogance but out of the deepest conviction.

His argument now becomes biographical. He declared that he received the gospel from the risen Christ at the time of his conversion.

Why is he so insistent on his independence from and yet oneness with the other apostles?

The false teachers seem to have maintained that he was simply an emissary of the true apostles, rather in the way Timothy and Titus acted on his behalf (1 Tim. 1:3; Titus 1:5), and that he had gone beyond his brief in the teaching on Christian freedom he had given in Galatia.

It would have been easy for visitors from Jerusalem to misrepresent things when they visited a place like Galatia. It was a long way from Jerusalem geographically and even further culturally. Here the local Christians would have great difficulty in verifying the facts about what was being preached and taught many miles away in Jerusalem.

Obviously then Paul himself had to answer these allegations. He shows that the contacts he had with the other apostles were few and far between in the years after his conversion and that there was no question of his receiving his gospel from them.

Moreover, when he did meet them, they recognised fully that his preaching among the Gentiles was completely authentic. He and they preached one and the same gospel. If there was any difference between them, it was in different spheres of service and not in any divergence in the content of their preaching.

As we have seen, even Paul's conflict with Peter at Antioch does not bring this oneness with the other apostles into question. There was no difference of theological convictions involved. In fact, Peter was guilty of actions that were contrary to convictions he and Paul held in common.

The issue at Corinth

In 2 Corinthians 10-13, Paul addresses the same question. His concern is clear but his passion does not seem to be quite so white-hot as in his letter to the Galatians.

Why was this? It was because the authenticity of the gospel was not immediately at stake here in the way it had been at Galatia. Who knows though what the ultimate consequences might have been if the attack on his apostleship had gone unchallenged?

It is worth mentioning that New Testament scholars are divided as to the unity of 2 Corinthians [1]. Some hold that these chapters are in fact part of another epistle to the same church, but there is general agreement that they are by Paul. The issue need not therefore concern us here. It is Paul who writes and it is to the Corinthians that the chapters were written. The focus of our interest then will be entirely on their actual contents.

We can see from these chapters that there were people

at Corinth reckoning themselves to be apostles. There is a good deal of discussion still about them and little general agreement as to who they were or what precisely they taught. There are however some things that are quite clear.

David Clines well sums up what we can learn about these 'false apostles':

> 'They were Jewish Christians (11:22f), visitors from outside Corinth (cf. 11:4), who came armed with letters of commendation (3:1), claiming for them a higher authority than Paul's (10:7). Their method of gaining adherents was to assert their own authority, no doubt with some eloquence (cf. 10:10; 11:6) and a great deal of mutual admiration (10:12), and to denigrate Paul before his converts (10:1f,10; 11:7, etc.). They were evidently not averse to receiving financial support from the church (11:12,20), yet behaved in a high- handed and insolent way toward it (11:20), and boasted of the Corinthians as if they were their own converts.' [2]

It seems then that it was not so much the gospel that was at stake here as the Christian lifestyle. These are in fact the two most important questions to ask about any preacher: does he preach the authentic message of God, and does his lifestyle support what he says?

The true apostles were responsible not only for laying a gospel foundation, but also for showing by their life quality the kind of standards a Christian should seek to maintain.

These false apostles were no doubt tarred with the worldly brush that characterized so many in the Corinthian church. In that church some were seeking a reputation for wisdom and there were people who valued the showy above the solid. The false teachers found a congenial human environment there.

Paul's defence here is quite different from what he says in the Galatian epistle. It is related much more to the quality of his life than to the evidence for his direct appointment to apostleship by the risen Christ. The situation was different, so the defence must be different.

He found the whole business distasteful. At one point he says, 'I hope you will put up with a little of my foolishness' (11:1). Later he writes, 'I have made a fool of myself, but you drove me to it' (12:11).

He focuses first of all on the fact that he shared God's jealousy for the purity of the church (11:1-4). He was very concerned that they should not be led astray from a pure and sincere devotion to Christ.

He might lack eloquence but he does have knowledge (11:5,6). He probably means that he has received the truth of the gospel from Christ. This then makes a point of contact with his argument in Galatians 1 and 2.

He has apparently been criticised for preaching and teaching without payment! Perhaps his critics were saying that somebody with the exalted status of an apostle would never do that. If so, how little they understood the principles of the kingdom of the lowly Jesus! Paul in fact sees this willingness rather as evidence of his true apostleship (11:7-15).

Then, in a particularly moving passage (11:16-33) he writes about his sufferings in the cause of Christ.

What a catalogue of pains, privations and persecutions! No charlatan would ever have been prepared to face such sufferings and endure them over so many years.

The passage is too long to quote but it is important to read it to feel the full force of it.

It is only after saying all this that Paul refers to his visions

(12:1-11) and the signs of an apostle (12:12), which were partly moral ('perseverance') and partly miraculous.

Without doubt this is where the 'false apostles' would have started!

The form the issue takes today

It might seem at first sight that there can be no parallel to Paul's defence of his apostleship as far as the modern church is concerned.

After all, most of us believe apostleship in this distinctive sense to have been a foundational rather than a continuing office in the Christian church [3]. We now have the apostolic testimony in written and therefore in permanent form in the New Testament.

Yet there is a parallel. The gospel is no less important today than it was in the first generation of the church's life.

We can learn from Paul that the gospel must not only be preached but defended.

If, in fact, a Christian preacher finds his preaching to be attacked, not because his presentation of it is dull, not because he has not found adequate illustrations of it, nor even because his sermons are too long (or even too short!) but essentially because of its gospel content, then it is not only legitimate but mandatory that he should defend it. An attack on the gospel is not simply an attack on its preacher but on the God who sent him.

At times too this will involve a defence of his call to serve God in a particular situation.

If it is being said that he should be replaced in the pulpit by somebody who will preach some form of Christianized humanism rather than the authentic gospel, he needs to speak up. He must, of course, be careful not to give the impression that his pride has been hurt, but there can be no question whatever of giving in without a fight when the gospel itself is at stake.

The gospel testimony depends in every age in large part on the quality of those who preach it.

It is not surprising then that a farmer or a clerk can get away with conduct that would immediately bring a minister into the public eye. The highlighting of the misdemeanours of a minister is in fact a kind of backhanded compliment to the gospel we preach, because it implies that it calls for high moral standards on the part of those who serve God in this way.

For a man whose moral testimony has been flawed in some serious way to try to insist on retaining his position in the church, or even to argue for it, is itself an undermining of the gospel. It is to reduce, in effect, the moral demands of the gospel which are implicit in the call to repentance.

Not only must our gospel be authentic, but our lives should provide credible illustrations of it.

References

1. For a survey of the arguments, see P. E. Hughes. *Paul's Second Epistle to the Corinthians*. New International Commentary on the New Testament. Grand Rapids. 1962; C. Kruse. *2 Corinthians*. Tyndale New Testament Commentary. Leicester. 1987
2. D. J. A. Clines. *A Bible Commentary for Today*. London. 1979. p.1480.
3. See P. R. Jones. '1 Corinthians 15:8: Paul the Last Apostle' in *Tyndale Bulletin 36*. Nottingham. 1985. pp. 3-34.

12

Setting Doctrine Right

Does it matter very much what we believe? Surely experience is more important than doctrine, isn't it?

Questions like this are being widely asked today. They are based on a serious misconception.

It is perfectly true that Christian experience is vitally important. The good news proclaimed in the New Testament is that sinful men and women may know the true and living God through Christ, that they may know him in actual daily life and experience.

Also of course it is possible to believe many right things and yet to be far from the kingdom of God because of wilful rejection of the gospel. Mere knowledge is not enough. As James puts it, 'You believe that there is one God. Good! Even the demons believe that - and shudder' (James 2:19).

But there is a vital link between doctrine and experience. The gospel calls us to put our faith in Jesus. If we are to do this, however, it is obvious that we must know something about him. We cannot trust in an empty name, but only in a real Person. For this trust to be real we need information about him - and that is doctrine.

If good doctrine is needed for genuine Christian faith it is also needed for true Christian growth. If growth in grace is based, as it is, on more intimate knowledge of Christ, we are going to need more understanding of who he is and of what he has done for us.

This is why it is so important for churches to be right in their understanding of Christian truth. If their members are going to become strong in the Lord the churches needs to be able to provide this good teaching. For this reason, if for no other, we all ought to be concerned about the kind of training ministers and other Christian workers receive.

It is not at all surprising that some of the infant churches of the apostolic period had theological problems. When the Holy Spirit brings us to the new birth, this affects every aspect of our personalities, but this does not mean we become perfect overnight, nor do we gain complete understanding all at once.

People reared outside the Christian faith often have a great deal to unlearn. This is to be expected, of course. After all, some of them have been thinking in a way foreign to biblical thinking for a very long time. They need to reconstruct their whole approach to life and to do so on the basis of the Scriptures. We do not always realise however that people brought up in Christian homes, who have attended fine evangelical churches for many years also have a lot to unlearn, but it is true.

It is not simply that we are all exposed to other influences as well, although of course we are. What we often forget is that God's truth meets resistance in the mind and heart of a non-Christian, even one exposed to Christian truth from his or her earliest days.

It is doubtful in fact whether any of us ever becomes totally free of non-Christian thinking, although this complete 'take-over' by the 'Christian mind' is certainly something for which we should earnestly seek. From the time of our conversion, we need to become life-long students of God's truth in his word.

In most of the churches to which Paul wrote there was a mixture of Jews and Gentiles. Some of the Gentiles would have a background of synagogue worship and teaching while others would not.

Each of these churches was founded on a common acceptance of the gospel. The initial teaching they were given by the apostles and their co-workers will have consisted of a fuller exposition of that gospel and some of its implications.

These implications were theological as well as practical.

Even the Jews in the churches had a lot to think about. They would need to review all they had learned about God from the synagogue teachers in the light of Christ. Without any doubt, they would begin to see much in the Old Testament from a new perspective.

If re-thinking was necessary for the Jews, how much more was this true for Gentiles who had never been inside a synagogue! The re-orientation they needed was simply massive.

What about the modern-day Christian?

We may not realise how unwilling we are to let go some of our precious prejudices! Our minds need to be open to all that God would teach us from his word. There can be no progress towards a God-honouring life without this.

What kinds of error was Paul particularly concerned about?

Error directly undermining the gospel

From the theological point of view, the young churches faced different problems.

Some of these arose from within their fellowship. Some of their people were puzzled about particular aspects of

Christian truth and they needed good clear teaching.

Other problems came from outside. Just as today Christians live in a theologically infected environment, so it was then. There were often people about who were anxious to teach them something other than the truth. The external threats of this sort were usually more radical than the internal.

This was true both in Galatia and at Colosse. In Galatia, as we have seen, it was the sufficiency of Christ's work that was under attack. At Colosse it was the significance of his person.

Christianity is Christ. The gospel we are called to declare does not consist of abstractions. It is about a person, and that person is Jesus, the Son of God.

The person and the work of Christ are both absolutely central to the gospel. If he had not been who he claimed to be, his death on the cross would have accomplished nothing for our salvation, and his resurrection would not have happened at all.

What then accounts for the difference in tone between Paul's letters to the Galatians and to the Colossians? The latter is calm in tone, while 'calm' is the last word that could be applied to the former!

The difference is due to the fact that the Galatians were showing signs of giving way to the heresy to which they were exposed, whereas the Colossians were not. In both letters Paul uses words often employed in military circles.

He tells the Colossians he admires their orderly ranks (Col. 2:5). They were standing fast in the good fight of the faith.

Not so the Galatians. He said to them that he was astonished they were so quickly deserting the true God and turning to a false gospel (Gal. 1:6), just like soldiers who were showing signs of defecting to the enemy.

In both cases Paul gave teaching to challenge the heresies and to build faith in the authentic gospel.

At Galatia, as we have seen already, he exalted the cross of Jesus. His atoning work on that cross was all-sufficient for the needs of everyone who would trust in him. God declares sinners righteous, not on the basis of their own efforts but through his own unmerited favour to them, to be received by simple faith.

What about Colosse? What was happening there?

It appears that in that part of Asia Minor Christ was being debased by false teachers. Who exactly they were is not clear and is still being debated by New Testament scholars.[1]

Some see them as Jews who were promoting a diluted version of the Christian faith.

For them, Christ was simply one among a whole series of mediators between God and the human race, and not a very exalted one at that. Of course, Jews accepted the existence of angels and so it was easy enough to fit another super-human figure into the system.

Others see them as Gentiles who came to Christianity from Middle Platonism. Philo was an important Jewish teacher in Alexandria, an older contemporary of the men of the New Testament. He was a Middle Platonist, combining Judaism with Platonic and Stoic elements. Middle Platonism existed in many different varieties, because it consisted of combinations of Plato's thought with other kinds of philosophy or with some religious ideas. (The philosopher Plato believed in a world beyond the one we can see, a world that affects our own world at every point.)

For one teacher the ingredients would be one part of Platonism to one of Aristotelianism, to another two of Platonism to one of Stoicism, and so on. Eventually the whole seething cauldron of ideas settled down into a new kind of 'authorised version' known as Neoplatonism.

If, as some scholars think, these heretics had started as Jews who followed Philo's ideas and were simply adding yet another element to the mixture, this time Christianity, this would probably explain all the features of it we can infer from Paul's attack on it in his letter.

The exact nature of the heresy may never be determined, and for our purposes it does not matter a great deal. What does matter is the kind of letter Paul wrote to the Colossians who were being assaulted by it.

What did Paul do? Just the opposite of what the heretics were doing. They were debasing Christ. He exalted him. Paul proclaimed that Jesus is the image of the Father. He asserted that he has the supremacy in every realm. Not only so but he has that supremacy because he deserves it. He deserves supremacy in the universe because he created it. He deserves supremacy in the new creation, the new society that is the church, because he died to save its people from their sins.

How could he do all this? Why, because of who he is. In him all the fullness of the Godhead (in other words, all that God is), dwells in bodily form.

What else do his people need then? Nothing! In him they receive everything they could possibly need. They are in fact complete in him, so he exhorts them to reject the heresy and to continue in the truth of Christ.

There is no doubt at all that the teaching Paul attacks in this epistle would have destroyed the gospel.

As Athanasius was later to see with crystal clarity, any reduction of the true and full deity of Jesus undermines the gospel. How can we be sure of the effectiveness of his work unless he is truly God as well as fully man?

This is still a live issue for Christ's church. In Britain and in some other western countries, Christians live in a society with many immigrants who are adherents of other religions. What is to be our attitude to such people?

Without doubt Christ's call to us is to show them his love in every way we can. Does this mean though that we are to treat their religions as on a par with the Christian faith? By no means!

Our Saviour showed real love and compassion to the Samaritans, and yet, when talking to a Samaritan woman, he said to her, 'You Samaritans worship what you do not know; we worship what we do know, for salvation is from the Jews' (John 4:22).

The uniqueness of Jesus is an embarrassment for those who profess to be Christians and yet who regard unity with other religions as important. It would seem to be quite impossible to teach that all religions are equally valid ways to God without surrendering not only the uniqueness of Christ's work but also of his person.

If there are other ways to God, other possible mediators between God and human beings, how can we possibly say that Jesus stands alone? If he has not made the only way to God, we can no longer believe him to be the incarnation of the only God there is.

If we give up this belief about him, we have given up the whole Christian faith, for Christianity is Christ.

It is so important for Christians to be instructed in the biblical teaching about the uniqueness of Christ. This teaching is very extensive and is to be found throughout the New Testament. In the pluralistic climate of today it is more important than ever for pastors to be sure there is enough concentration on it in the main preaching and teaching programme of the local church.

Error undermining the gospel by its implications

Christians tend to make a distinction between truths that are central to the Christian faith and those that are peripheral. The language Paul uses supports this, although, of course, this does not mean that any truth revealed by God is insignificant.

Writing to the Corinthians, he said to them, 'For what I received I passed on to you as of first importance: that Christ died for our sins according to the Scriptures, that he was buried, that he was raised on the third day according to the Scriptures' (1 Cor. 15:3,4).

If these gospel truths are central then there must be others that are less so. His references to baptism in the same epistle (1:13-17) certainly seem to suggest he treated the gospel he preached as more important than the rite that symbolised and sealed it. We can only speculate as to how he may have viewed our modern differences on minor matters of church government or of the fulfilment of biblical prophecy.

Gospel truth though was what he preached and what he would defend to the last ditch.

'Central', 'peripheral' - these seem valid distinctions, but do we not need a third category? There are some truths which, although not absolutely central, almost become so when the implications of their denial are faced.

An outstanding example of such a 'medial' truth is

found in 1 Corinthians 15:12-34. There were some at Corinth denying the resurrection of the dead. Later, in 2 Timothy 2:18, Paul refers to two men who 'say that the resurrection has already taken place, and they destroy the faith of some.'

Without doubt, Paul treated this kind of error seriously.

Why such teaching? It was very much in line with the general outlook of the Greeks. They thought matter was at least inferior to mind and some reckoned it to be evil. Probably these Christians simply thought the spirit would survive but the body would be gone for ever.

Did Paul teach anything that might have unintentionally encouraged this idea? Possibly. He believed and taught that Christians are already risen with Christ because they already have new life in him (Col. 3:1-4). This did not however do away with the future bodily resurrection, but rather guarantees it.

There are still theologians who hold that the Christian's present experience of spiritual resurrection is the only resurrection there is. This should be considered to be just as unacceptable now as Paul reckoned it then, and for much the same reasons. In 1 Corinthians 15, Paul takes time to deal with this issue fairly fully. He shows that a denial of the resurrection of the dead must, by the simple application of logic, undermine the gospel itself, for it must mean that Christ did not rise. His unstated assumption, of course, is that Jesus was a real man, as he undoubtedly was.

Here we see the importance of encouraging Christians to think through the theological implications of what they believe.

Take, for instance, the virgin birth of Christ.

This is not of course the same as the incarnation. The

latter is the fact that God became man in Christ, while the former is the method by which this was brought about. Although both facts are often denied together, there are some who believe in the incarnation but deny the virgin birth.

This denial can however raise all sorts of problems. Remember that, in the final analysis, the basis of our acceptance of the incarnation and of the virgin birth is one and the same - the testimony of God in Holy Scripture.

Errors denying the necessity of moral response to the gospel

Extreme antinomianism (the divorce of religion and morality) is regarded in the New Testament, and so in Paul's epistles, as a very serious error. Why?

Because it undermines the gospel, not so much in its theological content but in terms of its call for response on the part of the hearer. The gospel calls human beings to repentance and so this means that the sinner must begin to view his own personal sin with a new seriousness as something God hates and judges.

In Romans 6:1, 2, Paul asks, 'What shall we say, then? Shall we go on sinning, so that grace may increase? By no means! We died to sin; how can we live in it any longer?'

Paul did not waste time refuting errors nobody held. So there must have been some who were teaching that, because the grace of God covers all, sin does not matter. In fact, some were even, either mistakenly or maliciously, accusing him of teaching this (Rom. 3:8).

Now this is essentially a theological and not merely an ethical error. This is because in the New Testament ethical principles and precepts always rest on theological foundations.

An outstanding example of this is to be found in Romans 12:1,2, verses which are truly pivotal within their setting in this great Pauline epistle.

Paul has spent eleven chapters expounding the theology of the gospel. He has dealt in turn with sin and judgement, with justification (being put right with God) and with its many consequences in the life and destiny of the Christian, and then the special problem of Israel's apparent rejection in the light of their divine election.

He then says, 'Therefore, I urge you, brothers, in view of God's mercy, to offer your bodies as living sacrifices, holy and pleasing to God - this is your spiritual act of worship. Do not conform any longer to the pattern of this world, but be transformed by the renewing of your mind. Then you will be able to test and approve what God's will is - his good, pleasing and perfect will.' This is followed by many ethical injunctions.

'Therefore' plus the words, 'in view of God's mercy' underlines for us the connection between chapters 1 to 11 and what now follows.

It is God's mercy, expounded theologically in these chapters, that should prompt us, through gratitude, to a life of service to him, a life marked by qualities of godly character, that is, marks of Christ's own character.

To deny this union of doctrine and ethics, this wedding of the gospel and conduct, is undoubtedly a serious heresy. The modern church needs to reject such teaching just as decisively as Paul did.

References

1. See R. P. Martin. *Colossians: the Church's Lord and the Christian's Liberty.* Exeter. 1972. pp. 4-20

13

Handling Personalities and Parties

Churches are composed of human beings. That may be a trite truism, but it is important to remember it.

In theory the gospel unites people. Christ has brought all Christians to God through his atoning death. Because that death was for all believers without discrimination, we are brought together in a fellowship that finds its unity in the gratitude of all the members to him.

It does not always work out in practice, and yet it is really a denial of the gospel when it does not. We certainly need to realise this.

It is easy enough too to criticise other Christians and yet to be just as guilty ourselves. We may find the thought of apartheid in church life intolerable, but are we guilty of more informal discrimination in our own? How would somebody of a different colour or social class find your own church? The handshake at the church door is one thing, but the opened house may be quite another.

At Rome

As we have seen in a previous chapter, Paul addressed a situation at Rome where there were two tendencies. The evidence does not necessarily indicate two well-defined parties, but certainly there were two very different ways of thinking and acting. The 'weak' may have been mostly Jews, the 'strong' mostly Gentiles.

After discussing the main issue that threatened to divide them, Paul then says, 'Accept one another, then, just as Christ accepted you, in order to bring praise to God' (Rom. 15:7).

What is he really saying? He is asserting that the gospel is essentially a uniting message.

In one way, of course, it brings division, for, at the deepest spiritual level, it will divide us from those in our families and other social groups to which we belong who do not accept Christ. For some believers, this may be very costly. In fact, for some it has even led to their death.

In the gospel, though, we find a new family, a new society. In the gospel, Christ accepts us all without distinction. He makes no enquiry as to whether we belong to the 'right' group. He spent a good deal of his time with people other folk despised. We should be just as wholehearted and as wide-ranging in our acceptance of others in him.

At Philippi

Most of us think of the Philippian church as a very fine one. There is good cause for this.

If, as somebody has said, 'the last thing to be sanctified in a Christian is his pocket,' then these Philippian Christians were well sanctified. They had shown much thoughtful generosity to Paul. In fact one of the main purposes of the writing of his letter to them was to express his thanks for their open-handedness towards him (Phil. 4:10-19).

There is however one verse in the letter that points to a less than idyllic situation. In chapter 4, verse 2, he says, 'I plead with Euodia and I plead with Syntyche to agree with each other in the Lord.'

When Paul first arrived in Philippi, he preached to a group of women who gathered by the riverside on Sabbath days to pray there. There must therefore have been few male Jews in Philippi.

We know nothing about these two women apart from this passage. They may well have been early converts, and, as verse 3 indicates, they contended at his side (in ways unspecified in the passage) in the cause of the gospel. It is clear that Paul had valued their fellowship in the work.

Something had gone wrong. There had been a rift between them.

What was the cause of this breach in their fellowship? This is never spelled out. The Bible does not minister to our curiosity! It did not need to be specified for the Philippians, of course, because they would be well aware of it.

It was probably quite a serious quarrel. Some commentators have pointed out that Paul uses the verb translated 'plead' twice in this passage, once in connection with each name. This suggests that these two women were far enough apart to make it seem necessary to address them separately rather than together.

What is he asking them to do? To agree 'in the Lord'. This is a most significant phrase. They had both been won by the same gospel; they had both laboured for the extension of the same kingdom; they were both in fellowship with the same Christ. How wrong that they should not get on with each other!

Paul could easily have addressed to them the appeal he had made to the Romans: 'Accept one another, then, just as Christ accepted you, in order to bring praise to God' (Rom. 15:7). Whether in terms of warring parties or of clashing personalities, the challenge was to accept the implications of the gospel and to welcome and love one another for Christ's sake.

In view of this, it is interesting to note the repetition of the word 'all' in Philippians 1:3-8. This cannot be accidental. It comes so often that it seems Paul is making a special point. He prayed for all of them, loved all of them, shared in God's grace with all of them, longed to see all of them.

Was he suggesting that he would never be partial, and that he would never take sides, but rather that his whole concern was with reconciliation? If so, when the letter was read out in the church, the thrust of this passage should have got home to Euodia and Syntyche before ever they heard chapter four read.

It is his reference to a mutual sharing of grace which is most significant. If Christ has brought us, through grace, to himself, he has therefore brought us to one another and we should show this in our attitudes and actions.

Before we leave the Philippian situation, it is worth noting that this was probably a comparatively small church. Serious personality clashes can more easily arise and become a major factor in the life of a small church.

You see, if you belong to a large church, you may be able to choose more easily those with whom you have the closest fellowship. You may have some kind of antipathy against one of your brothers or sisters in Christ, but without this coming to the notice of others. It may not even concern you very much. After all, he or she sits in a different part of the building, and goes to a different house group.

But it should concern you! Spiritually any breach of fellowship is serious. Whether in a small church or a large, we all sit together at the Lord's Table, and we should be in love and fellowship with all who sit there with us.

At Corinth

A troubling situation had arisen at Corinth. Tendencies to division there had gone much further than they had at Rome or at Philippi. Definite parties had arisen.

There appear to have been four parties, each proud of the name of a particular teacher (1 Cor. 1:12). Three of these were prominent Christians, Paul, Apollos and Cephas (Peter). The fourth was the name of Christ himself.

We might be inclined to exonerate the Christ party from blame, but we would be wrong to do so. In fact, they were probably saying, 'We belong to Christ - and the rest of you do not!' If so, they were the worst party of them all. Nothing is a greater breach in the worldwide church than the claim of a group that its members alone belong to Christ's church, to the temple of the Holy Spirit, to God's family.

To explore the varying characteristics of these parties is irrelevant to our purpose just now. Have you noticed that in fact Paul does not do so himself? What each of them stood for may have been of some significance, both to them and also to the parties that differed from them, but not compared with the fact that they existed at all. This shows very clearly how troubled he was about this party-spirit.

His concern is shown in a number of ways. It is particularly worth noting that this is the very first issue with which he deals in his first extant letter to this church. The church at Corinth had a number of problems, and Paul deals with quite a number of them, but it is this he addresses first of all.

Not only so, but he devotes four chapters to the matter. This is a fuller treatment than any of their other problems receives from him.

How wise he was too in the way he addressed the issue of the parties! After telling them what he had learned about the situation (1 Cor. 1:10-12), he went straight on, in verses 13 to 17, to criticise the Paul party. 'Is Christ divided? Was Paul crucified for you? Were you baptised into the name of Paul?' and so on.

This is very telling. It shows that he was just as concerned about the existence of a party using his name as he was about the others. He was certainly not going to side with this party in its disputes with the others.

It is true that his reference to the powerful signs for which Jews seek could be a glance at the Peter-party, which was probably largely or exclusively Jewish. His allusions to wisdom too may relate particularly to one party, the group that followed the eloquent Apollos.

If however miracles and wisdom had become causes of pride to these two parties, he was right to emphasise his own simple preaching of the gospel of the cross. This is no criticism of either Apollos or Peter but rather of the parties gathered round their names.

Then he moves on to deal with the worldly pride in man which exalts the name of a human leader. He does this by selecting his own name and that of Apollos.

It is most noteworthy that he asks, 'What, after all, is Apollos? And what is Paul?' (3:5). Not who, but what! To put the question in this way was almost insulting, but, of course, to himself as well as to Apollos.

Paul and Apollos are only servants of God. Each has his own function, but they are simply servants. They have themselves been given no cause for pride, for, as Paul points out, God has in fact allowed them to go through all kinds of privations and suffering for the sake of the gospel. Men may be exalting them, but if God is showing them his favour it seems to be by abasing them!

Lest perhaps they should go to the opposite extreme of their present outlook and ignore their God-appointed teachers altogether, Paul concludes this particular section of his letter by calling on them to follow his way of life (1 Cor. 4:14-17).

He was their father in Christ, for it was through his preaching that so many of them had been brought to faith in Christ. A human father is called to teach his children not only by word but by example, and this was true also of Paul, their spiritual father. They were certainly not meant to form a party round his name, but they were to take his teaching and his manner of life seriously.

His relations with individual Christians

There are two incidents in the life of Paul which are often the subject of criticism on the ground that he showed himself, on both occasions, to be an awkward character. Both incidents took place at Antioch, the great mission centre from which he went out on each of his three recorded missionary journeys.

The first is the confrontation with Peter to which he refers in Galatians 2. We have already considered the reason for this in an earlier chapter.

We have, of course, no record of this event from Peter himself. Paul's account indicates however that in his mind its importance lay in the conduct of Peter which was inconsistent with the gospel they both believed.

Antioch, where it happened, was the place where, for the first time, large numbers of Gentiles had been won for Christ. How important then, at such a place and at such a time, that the way the Christian leaders acted should show very clearly the principles of God's grace in the gospel!

Peter was failing to make this kind of witness. He had been eating with the Gentiles, but when Hebrew Christians who were close to James in Jerusalem arrived on the scene he gave this up. He evidently thought they would disapprove of what he had been doing.

What would his actions suggest to the observer? That Jews and Gentiles were not meant by God to be together in fellowship. They might even have suggested that God has one way of acceptance for the Jew and quite another for the Gentile.

Paul's critical comment to Peter seems, therefore, to be wholly justified. More than that, was this not exactly what was needed in the circumstances?

The other occasion is recorded in Acts 15:36-40.

Here there was sharp disagreement between Paul and Barnabas. The question at issue concerned the membership of the team for the Second Missionary Journey. Barnabas wished to take John Mark, who was in fact his cousin, but Paul did not think this wise, as he had deserted them during the course of the First Journey.

Those who are critical of Paul sometimes take issue with his unwillingness to take Mark, saying that he should have been given another chance. After all, many of us have needed a second chance and some more senior Christian has graciously given it to us. Why then was Paul so hard on John Mark?

There is however an important factor that can easily be overlooked. Preachers of the gospel have the great responsibility of representing the Christian lifestyle in their conduct as well as proclaiming the Christian gospel with their lips.

If Mark had left the work without a godly motive, and Paul was not assured that he would not do so again, this would itself be a bad testimony to the gospel. Paul could not risk this. He had to consider the wider needs of the work.

It is not easy to deal with situations of this kind, where the needs of the work and the encouragement of the individual appear to clash, but God is able to give his servants wisdom.

At times somebody who has failed in one sphere and yet who has learned from this may be better used in a different kind of Christian work. It is a joy to find Mark given honourable mention, and mentioned specifically as a Christian worker, in two of Paul's later epistles (Col. 4:10; 2 Tim. 4:11).

Most critics of Paul however fasten not so much on the division of opinion but on the spirit shown by the two men. Luke says, 'They had such a sharp disagreement that they parted company' (Acts 15:39). These words certainly seem to indicate that some heat was generated between them. We need not rush to the defence of Paul, for the inspiration of his writings is no guarantee of perfect Christian conduct. He was a man of strong convictions and may have lost his temper during the argument.

Having said this, we also ought to point out, in fairness to Paul, that his letters are full of warm, brotherly and encouraging comments about Christians he knows and with whom he has worked. His letter to Philemon is a model of courtesy. In all these letters he shows himself to be a true Christian gentleman.

He may not have been perfect, but his life showed many marks of the fruit of the Spirit and must have been a great challenge to his converts, as it is also to us today.

Our modern situation

It is so easy for us to divide from other believers, in spirit, if not actually within our church fellowships.

Such divisions may still take place, as they did in Paul's day, over matters that are secondary or because of personality clashes or party-spirit. Such tendencies by no means belong only to the past.

In fact, in this ecumenical age, it is often forgotten that divisions within a local church are in fact a much greater scandal than denominational divisions. Non-Christians are not always aware of what goes on in the heady sphere of church politics. If there is trouble in the church at the end of the street, however, news of it tends to spread quickly.

We live in a world which is full of fractured relationships. This is true between nations and within nations, between families and within families, and in countless other ways. If all items reflecting this were to be removed from our daily newspapers, how much thinner they would be!

In our own locality we should be an object-lesson in human relationships, an example of the fact that Christ unites all kinds of people in himself through the gospel.

All too often we are guilty of making the gospel seem less credible because we do not love each other enough. This ought not to be.

If you find yourself at odds with another Christian, you need to bring that other person, and, not least, your attitude towards him or her, to God's throne in prayer. So often, it is at the place of prayer that love, not only for Christ, but for others, is rekindled.

14

Establishing High Standards

Paul had a lot of ethical issues to deal with.

Sometimes this was because a church had written to him about them or because he had been told about the situation in the church and so felt the need to take the initiative and give counsel. Both these factors lie behind the writing of his First Letter to the Corinthians.

In the ethical confusion of modern life there are many questions we might have in our minds as we approach Paul's letters. Not all of them will be dealt with explicitly in those letters, but even if they are not we may be able to discern principles of abiding validity.

In every age, churches are bound to be influenced by what is happening in the world around them. The ethical confusion of our society has not left our churches unscathed.

Can we find guiding lines in these letters, principles that will also be of service to us in our local churches? What are the ethical implications of the gospel itself? Are these spelled out in his letters, or do we simply have to infer them? Are there times when they are simply taken for granted?

In a great but neglected passage in Paul's letter to Titus, he says something most important: 'For the grace of God that brings salvation has appeared to all men. It teaches us to say "No" to ungodliness and worldly passions, and to live self-controlled, upright and godly lives in this present age, while we wait for the blessed hope - the glorious appearing of our great God and Saviour, Jesus Christ, who gave himself for us to redeem us from all wickedness and to purify for himself a people that are his very own, eager to do what is good' (Titus 2:11-14).

So, this passage tells us, there is a moral purpose to the death of Christ. This means then that the gospel itself actually teaches us the basic truth that a Christian is to be different. To be redeemed by God is to become godly.

Presumably basic principles were taught orally to Christians when they were brought to Christ. 'The apostles' teaching' (Acts 2:42) will certainly have been moral as well as doctrinal.[1] We would therefore expect to encounter such principles in the written material from time to time.

We would expect principles of this kind to be both general and far-reaching. If they were, they could integrate the various ethical injunctions of the epistles.

This is in fact what we do find.

The Christian life does not flout standards God has already set.

What about the Decalogue, the Ten Commandments? These are the basis of so much ethical teaching in the Old Testament. Do they have any place for the Christian?

Paul certainly did not regard keeping the Law a means of salvation. This does not mean however that he felt free to ignore it altogether. We should not in fact expect this, for the God who gave the Ten Commandments has not changed his moral stance. The Christian faith is not libertarian, even though it has sometimes been treated as if it is, both in theory and in practice.

Are you in any doubt about this? If so, a study of the

Epistle to the Ephesians should soon dispel these doubts.

In this letter, Paul quotes the Fifth Commandment (Eph. 6:1-3) and it is clear he meant his readers to take it seriously.

It is however much more than a matter of one direct quotation. If you go through the epistle, you will find several of the other commandments represented in some form or another. They may not be quoted but it looks as if Paul is using them as moral standards. It would be a valuable exercise to go through the letter to see how many of them you can find. You can check your findings by consulting the footnote below. [2]

His epistles are in fact full of instructions of a moral nature, many of which rest on the fundamental standards of godly morality indicated in the commandments of the Decalogue.

If the Law has a continuing function - as it has - it is because it reveals the character of God and his norms for human life, which the Christian, through gratitude to Christ, seeks to embrace and express in the practical affairs of life.

The Christian life is a life out of death

In Romans 6, Paul demonstrates that the Christian ethic is grounded in the Christian gospel. In this great chapter, we can see that death and resurrection are not only the heart of the Christian gospel; they are also the heart of the Christian life.

What does he mean when he talks about Christians dying and rising again with Christ? Is it simply a matter of analogy? Jesus died and rose again physically, and so we may think of our refusal to live the old life and our commitment to the new life as a kind of death and resurrection. Is this it?

If it is merely an analogy, it lacks real theological significance. A truth can be illustrated by something taken from an entirely different subject. That is why it is so dangerous to base an argument on an illustration.

The relationship between Christ's physical death and resurrection and our spiritual death and resurrection is in fact far more than a simple comparison. Without the death and resurrection of Jesus himself there can be none for us. It is actually out of the death and resurrection of Jesus that our own death to sin and new life in God come.

This must be so, for everything in the Christian life is based on what Jesus has himself done for us. If he had not died for us, there would be no eternal life for us in heaven, and moreover no new life on earth either.

Also we need to consider carefully the relevance of union with Christ. What he has done for us is valueless until the Holy Spirit joins us to him.

By this union, the benefits of that death and resurrection can flow through to us, and so we experience God's forgiveness. Also his death and resurrection find reproduction in us through our union with him, a real break with the past (which is what a death is) and a real embracing of God's will for our daily life becoming gloriously possible.

Union with Christ is then the link between the Christian gospel and the Christian life that is rooted and grounded in it.

Because, in the eternal mind of God, those of us who believe were one with Christ when he died and rose again, he took us with him down into death and up into newness of life. All this is translated into experience by the grace of God when, in the new birth, we are united to Christ in practical experience. As Paul himself shows us in Romans 6, it is symbolized in baptism.

That is why it is such a mistake to set salvation through justification over against salvation by union. These are the two halves of one fact, distinguishable but indivisible.

This means, of course, that although the Christian deeply respects the Law of God, the Christian ethic is not grounded in legalism. In the gospel we are delivered from the self-dependence of legalism into the Christ-dependence of grace.

The Holy Spirit in the Christian life

Many ethical teachers have stressed the great importance of motive in morality. Jesus taught his disciples the importance not simply of outward acts but of the condition of the heart (Matt. 5:21,22,27,28; 15:1-20).

But what is a motive? An attitude, of course, and that is obviously important. If our attitude is wrong, our action may be right in other ways, but it is nevertheless gravely deficient. But is a motive more than an attitude?

Yes. Remember that the words 'motive' and 'motion' are connected! So it is also a driving force, an inner power, a dynamic that moves a person forward in a certain direction.

What is the driving force in a Christian's life? We should not ask what but who? It is a Person, the Holy Spirit.

Does this mean then that Paul is operating with two different principles in his thinking and teaching about the Christian life? Does he think at one time (say, in Romans 6), in terms of death and resurrection, while at another (say, in Romans 8), in terms of the inner dynamic of the Holy Spirit?

The very way the question is put points to the answer. Romans 6 and 8 are not just examples taken at random but are the classic passages in his writings dealing with these two principles. Not only so, but they are close together in the same epistle.

The fact of the matter is that death and resurrection with Christ on the one hand and walking in the Spirit on the other are vitally and intimately connected. It is in fact the Holy Spirit who unites us to Christ, the crucified and risen Christ, and who then becomes the vital motivating power within us for Christian living. The work of the Spirit is, in this as in all else, an application of the work of Christ.

This means that Romans 6 and 8 could not have been reversed. Christ's work is the substructure, the Spirit's the superstructure, of the Christian life. What Christ has done historically, judicially and finally, the Holy Spirit applies to us as individuals in terms of bringing us to the new birth and working within us to make us like Christ.

The cross and the empty tomb precede Pentecost. We may say reverently that we are dependent on what the Holy Spirit does, but also that he is himself dependent on what Christ has already done.[3] We cannot drive a wedge between the Son and the Spirit, for Paul never does this.

Christ accepted the cross long before he was crucified. We may say, in a sense, that spiritually he was living a crucified and risen life throughout his ministry. He also lived in constant dependence on the Holy Spirit.

Can we see, through Paul's teaching, that we need to regard ourselves as crucified and yet risen with Christ? We then can discover, also through his teaching, that we can depend on the Holy Spirit indwelling us to reproduce this lifestyle in our characters and conduct.

What is it that the Holy Spirit produces in the Christian life? Because he is the Spirit of union with Christ, he produces the fruit of Christ's own character in us. This is what the fruit of the Spirit is (Gal. 5:22,23).

The greatest of these qualities is love, and Paul never

tires of extolling and commending and encouraging love. 1 Corinthians 13 is, of course, his greatest passage on this theme.

The deepening of repentance and faith

In the gospel there is a call for repentance and faith. These are the two sides of the experience of conversion, or, we may put it, they represent a death and a resurrection, the ending of an old life and the beginning of a new one.

Paul's letters to the Colossians and to the Ephesians contain many moral exhortations. Two brief passages are however pivotal. Not only are they important in themselves; they are most illuminating when taken together.

In both passages Paul uses the removal of soiled clothing and its replacement by clean garments as an illustration of his thought.

To the Colossians, he says, 'Do not lie to each other, since you have taken off your old self with its practices and have put on the new self, which is being renewed in knowledge in the image of its Creator' (Col. 3:9,10).

To the Ephesians his word is, 'You were taught, with regard to your former way of life, to put off your old self, which is being corrupted by its deceitful desires, to be made new in the attitude of your minds, and to put on the new self, created to be like God in true righteousness and holiness' (Eph. 4:22-24).

The two passages taken together suggest that the initial act of repentance and faith is to be taught as the pattern for the whole of life. As we have received Christ Jesus as Lord, so we are to continue to live in him (Col. 2:6). The principle of our beginning is also to be the principle of our continuance, with the implication of constant deepening.

Turning my back on sin and turning my face towards Jesus, the great object of my faith - this is to be not only what happens in the decisive moment of my conversion, but thereafter in every moment. It is to become the habit of my life.

What truly good news this is, for sin is for ever worthless and Christ for ever worthy!

Again this shows the basic character of the gospel, but not only so. It shows it to be not only fundamental but also comprehensive. It is not only the basis of the Christian life; it includes everything the Christian life is or can ever become.

No wonder that in heaven the redeemed eternally pour out their praises to the crucified and risen Christ! Everything precious to them that they have received from God through his generosity, everything precious to God that they have been able to offer him through his grace, all this is the product of that cruel cross and that glorious victory.

Glory be to Jesus!

The ethical teaching of Paul

What has this to do with problems Paul faced in the churches? A very great deal, for he was guided by the gospel in all he wrote to churches on ethical issues.

We do not know how much he knew about some of them. Certainly he had visited some after their establishment, he had sent members of his team to visit others, he had received visitors from others, and from the Corinthians at least he had received correspondence.

His moral teaching is usually crystal clear. It is evident that he believed the church, in virtue of its redemption by Christ, to be different from the world which was its environment, and that it needed to demonstrate this difference in the daily lives of its members.

Notice what he has to say in Philippians 3:18-20: 'For, as I have often told you before and now say again even with tears, many live as enemies of the cross of Christ. Their destiny is destruction, their god is their stomach, and their glory is in their shame. Their mind is on earthly things. But our citizenship is in heaven.'

Why tears? Because, as the context shows, these were professing Christians and yet their manner of living demonstrated that they were without spiritual life.

When giving teaching on family and sexual ethics he relied very much on the Old Testament. This dependence is not always spelled out, but there is a great deal in the ethical sections of the epistles which could be documented from the pages of the Old Testament. We have seen this already in connection with the Ten Commandments and the letter to the Ephesians.

There is plenty of evidence for standard ethical teaching of new converts within the pages of the New Testament, and, in fact, in Paul's letters (e.g. in Rom. 6:17).

This teaching, given presumably from the very beginning under the authority of the apostles (Acts 2:42), will have brought out the implications of the new life in Christ for fundamental human relationships (Eph. 5:21-6:9; Col. 3:18-4:1).

Such teaching, of course, presupposes that the church is a community of the redeemed, belonging together because all belong to Christ. As we see from a non-Pauline letter (1 Peter 3:1ff.), it did take account of the possibility of one partner to a marriage being converted while the other was not.

In fact, in relation to marriage all sorts of issues would arise and many of these were apparently referred to in the letter the Corinthians wrote to Paul. He replies to them in 1 Corinthians 7.

Here we see another factor in Paul's ethical decisions. He is aware of the moral teaching of Christ. When, in 1 Corinthians 7:10, 12, 25 (cf. 9:14), he writes of commands as coming from the Lord, he has in view teaching given by Jesus during his earthly ministry.[4]

Because his readers had accepted Christ in the gospel, the Saviour's teaching was important for them. As gospel people, they would be most grateful to him for giving his life for them. So this means that they would take Paul's teaching with great seriousness, hearing in it the imperious and yet winsome tones of their Divine Saviour.

If, after reading the ethical sections of Paul's letters, you were to turn to the Gospels and read what the Lord Jesus had to say on these same issues, there is no doubt Paul would have been glad.

References

1. See A. M. Hunter. *Paul and his Predecessors*. New revised edn. London. 1961. pp. 52-57, 128-130.
2. For the Seventh Commandment, see Eph. 5:3, for the Eighth, Eph. 4:28, for the Ninth, Eph. 4:25, and for the Tenth, Eph. 5:5
3. I have tried to address this issue in my article, 'The Significance of Pentecost in the History of Salvation' in *The Scottish Bulletin of Evangelical Theology* 4:2. Edinburgh. Autumn 1986. pp. 97-107
4. See A. M. Hunter. *op.cit*. pp. 45-51, 126-128.

15

Encouraging Church Order

All living things have both vitality and structure.

This is true even of the simplest organism. In fact, the very word 'organism,' connected as it is with 'organization,' suggests structure. It is true of the plant, of the animal, of human beings; it is also true of societies, whether of ants or of people.

Vitality itself is not enough. Energy uncontrolled, unchannelled, will be dissipated and wasted. Even the machine requires order, the train needs lines, the motor-car a road, the ship the water surface and rudder, the aeroplane a joystick and ailerons.

Order itself is not enough. Coleridge's *Ancient Mariner* was not happy when he likened his vessel to 'a painted ship upon a painted ocean'. It was motionless for lack of wind. A dead plant or animal, a lifeless human being, a moribund society, a 'church' without the Spirit - these are all sad to behold.

Now a Christian church is a form of society. It is a phenomenon capable of sociological investigation and analysis, although at the same time a Divine institution.

Some churches seem to major on structure, others on vitality.

Paul's letters were written to young churches charged with spiritual life. Some of the energy was being dissipated however and in his letters he seeks to encourage structures which would channel that spiritual energy. He knew this would make ultimately for more effective gospel witness.

How did he do this? We can gather this chiefly from his dealings with three churches.

Ordering the Church at Corinth

1 Corinthians 11-14 is particularly concerned with order. His comments on church discipline, both in 1 Corinthians 5 and 2 Corinthians 2, are also relevant. We will look though at the four continuous chapters first.

Paul deals first with the question of head covering (1 Cor. 11:2-16).

The passage contains a number of interpretation problems. It seems, however, most likely that Christian women at Corinth, rejoicing in their freedom in Christ, were coming to worship without veils, and in this way offending against what their society regarded as proper for a virtuous woman.

Paul approaches the matter from two angles. He maintains that God has established both order and inter-dependence. This gives his teaching beautiful balance and clears him of the male chauvinism of which he has sometimes been accused.

In God's ordering of things, Paul says, even Christ submits to God. When we consider the teaching of the New Testament, including Paul himself, about the deity of Jesus, this is a most significant and moving fact. Christ took on servanthood when he became man, and so there is revealed to us that most astonishing of attributes - the humility of God (Phil. 2:5-8)!

In responding to the gospel, Christians have recognized the authority of Christ, and we gladly place ourselves under that authority. In entering the marriage relationship, a woman recognises the headship of her husband in the new family just beginning, and most women gladly do so.

This does not mean any intrinsic inferiority. The Son of God was in no way inferior to his Father. Willing submission to an equal is much more likely to be a sign of a person's intrinsic worth than the opposite, for it is the expression of high moral qualities.

Paul now goes on to write of the inter-dependence of men and women. Just as the first woman would not have existed at all without the prior existence of the man, for she was formed from him, so no subsequent man would exist without the prior existence of a woman, for he is born from her.

If any man is ever tempted to look down on women, let him ponder the place his mother has had in his life, not only in the care and love she has given him, but in carrying him within her for nine months and bringing him to the birth!

We may ask whether the head covering retains anything of its symbolic significance for human society in our world today? In some places, yes; in most places, no.

However we view the issue in its cultural bearing in Paul's world and in ours, there is no doubt that Paul's teaching here is based on two abiding principles, ordered headship and mutual dependence. Applications may vary from society to society, but these principles abide, and in a godly marriage and a biblical church they will be clearly seen.

Next comes the gospel ordinance of the Lord's Supper.

Paul was distressed at the greed and drunkenness which apparently marred its observance at Corinth. This was a shame on the name of the Christ they met to worship.

The Corinthian Christians had not understood, or at least, adequately appreciated the meaning of the Supper. It was to commemorate and give thanks for Christ's death, the most gracious act in the history of the world, calculated to move his people to the depths of their being.

How unthinkable then that they should act so offensively and so irreverently on such an occasion! It was not surprising that God had acted in judgement on some of them.

Paul makes it clear that each person was responsible for his or her attitude and demeanour at the Supper. There must be seriousness in recognition of the meaning of the Feast. There must be a spirit of reverence for God and of love and courtesy towards brothers and sisters in the one body of Christ.

After this comes a long section on spiritual gifts.

It is clear they were much in evidence at Corinth and were a major feature of their times of worship. They needed guidance as to their use.

Some commentators take it from the opening verses of chapter 12 that somebody at Corinth had actually said in a service of worship the horrifying words, 'Jesus be cursed!' We cannot be sure of this, but if so, it was presumably when he had lost control of what he was saying.

Paul sees this kind of thing, whether actual or hypothetical, as in some way continuous with their former experiences of pagan worship. Possibly the feature common to both was undisciplined frenzy.

By contrast, the confession that Jesus is Lord immediately introduces the principle of order, for to confess a Lord is to profess submission to authority. This is a mark of the authentic work of the Holy Spirit. So then true spirituality and order are not enemies but friends.

When a person becomes a Christian by responding to the gospel, the Holy Spirit comes to indwell him or her. This however is no recipe for individualism. The Spirit also unites the new Christian with other believers, and constitutes the whole group as the body of Christ. A body is structured; it is an organism.

This means then that to be in Christ, to be indwelt by the Spirit, is not just of immense individual significance. It is also a social fact.

Paul lists different types of Christian workers who were God's gifts to his church. Notice here his use of numbers, when, in 1 Corinthians 12:28, he says, 'And in the church God has appointed first of all apostles, second prophets, third teachers, then workers of miracles,' etc.

Apostles stand at the head of his list. Why? They were taught by Jesus and commissioned to preach and teach the gospel at the initial stage of the church's life. They were God's human agents through whom the church was established on a proper foundation and got its theological bearings.

Prophets and teachers, the other two numbered gifts, are also people of the word.

So, when he says, in verse 30, 'But eagerly desire the greater gifts', it is clear he is writing about those designated by number. How otherwise could the Corinthians have been sure of their relative values?

What then is the significance of this? That the word of God has to have a place of high importance in the church of Christ, a place well beyond that accorded to the gifts of miracles, healing, administration and tongues mentioned in the same passage.

The word of God, then, and especially the apostolic word, has a very special place in the church. It is through it

God teaches and therefore orders the life of the local fellowship (Col. 3:16ff.). At its heart, as Paul indicates in 1 Corinthians 15:3,4, is the gospel, the message of Christ crucified (compare what he says in 1:18, 23; 2:2).

So much meantime for the ordering of the church, but what about its vitality? What is the living quality that is to unite all the members and to express itself in everything the church does?

It is love. Paul extols this in chapter 13. Without it every gift is useless and even counter-productive.

He then goes on to discuss prophecy and tongues. He now introduces the further important principle of edification. To edify is, of course, to build. This criterion must be applied to everything in a service. If it does not build the church it should have no place, and to build the church means to encourage holiness, to stimulate love for Christ and for others, to promote service, to glorify Christ as the members grow up in him together.

Now Paul was convinced that understandable words are God's means of building the church in its services, and that in this connection anything not understood or not heard is valueless or even counter-productive.

He applies this to tongue-speaking. This can do nothing for the church unless it is interpreted. In fact, if an unbeliever comes in and hears words that mean nothing to him, the effect may be to confirm him in his rebellion against God and so in God's judgement on him rather than to lead him to trust the Saviour. Incredibly it even seems several were speaking in tongues at once!

Prophets too should speak in turn, for similar reasons. Paul had said, 'But everyone who prophesies speaks to men for their strengthening, encouragement and comfort' (1

Cor. 14:3), and this speaking in turn was 'so that everyone may be instructed and encouraged' (1 Cor. 14:31). Such ministries of instruction and encouragement are always edifying.

We should note especially that he says, 'If anybody thinks he is a prophet or spiritually gifted, let him acknowledge that what I am writing to you is the Lord's command. If he ignores this, he himself will be ignored' (1 Cor. 14:37,38). This means then that apostolic truth is the test of anything that professes to be prophetic truth. That apostolic truth we now have in the New Testament.

There is good reason to be concerned about a church if it places greater emphasis on special utterances in a service or meeting than on the written word of God.

It is in this context that Paul exhorts women to be silent. The way he puts it suggests to some commentators, and to the present writer, that some of them were asking questions in the church services, so introducing another disorderly feature into things.

Incomprehensible languages, speakers vying at the same time for the attention of the hearers, women calling out questions - what bedlam! No wonder Paul is so insistent on proper order!

Finally, at the very end of this section, he says, 'Therefore, my brothers, be eager to prophesy, and do not forbid speaking in tongues. But everything should be done in a fitting and orderly way.'

Even in chapter 16, where he is writing about the collection for the poor Christians in Jerusalem, he recommends planning and order.

Nobody with knowledge of the contemporary church scene can doubt the relevance of these principles today. We must remember that the Holy Spirit is the author both of spiritual vitality and of proper structure in the church. One without the other is a recipe either for death or for disaster.

The disciplinary issue of which Paul writes in 1 Corinthians 5 is incest. He is clearly appalled that the church has taken no action, for, as he says, it would have scandalised even unbelievers.

If the gospel calls for repentance, this means Christians should have different standards from the world. Where it is scandalously evident that a church member is following a lifestyle incompatible with the gospel he professes, the church has no alternative but to remove him from its fellowship.

This is no easy matter and can raise major problems, even legal difficulties. Prayer, a penitent attitude on the part of the whole church (which is entirely composed of sinners), eager concern not only to bring those concerned to repentance but also to help them with the practical consequences of their actions, will test in a radical way the true Christian quality of the church.

There must be discipline, for only in this way can the world and the church be seen to be distinct, underlining the gospel call to repentance. If however the church acts harshly, it has negated the very point discipline is meant to emphasize, namely that the church is meant to be different from the world.

There is difference of opinion as to whether or not the man referred to in 2 Corinthians 2 is the same as in 1 Corinthians 5. All the major commentaries on 2 Corinthians deal with the arguments for and against this.

For our purpose it matters little, for the main point is that he has evidently been disciplined for something. It is also clear he has shown real sorrow. Paul must have known there was evidence of repentance, for he calls the church to forgive and comfort him.

Here again we see how the gospel ruled Paul's thinking. It calls for repentance. When this is evident in an offender, he is to be forgiven and accepted, for he has shown the presence of God's grace in his life by his repentance, in other words by responding within God's own terms in the gospel.

Ordering the church at Ephesus

The church at Ephesus was one of the most privileged of New Testament churches. Not only did it have a longer ministry from Paul than he was able to give any other church, but also periods of ministry from Apollos, Priscilla and Aquila and the apostle John. It was probably the first recipient of all or most of the Johannine literature and also of the Epistle to the Ephesians.

Timothy was there as a legate of the apostle, commissioned to put things in order at the church in the way Paul himself would have done had he been there.

In his second letter to him, Paul concentrates largely on encouraging Timothy himself, but the first deals with many issues of church order, so many that we cannot look in detail at them all.

He writes of the prayer-life of the church (1 Tim. 2:1-8), and clearly implies that it should be wide. He urges this 'first of all'.

What would he think of modern inward-looking churches who have practically abandoned intercession at their regular services? Our gospel witness in the world is to be accompanied by earnest prayer for peaceable conditions.

He writes about women, urging modesty of dress. (Do not forget that men can dress immodestly too!)

His words about the need for women to be silent and his apparent ban on their teaching men has been discussed endlessly, especially in modern times.

It is tempting to regard it as cultural, and so as appropriate in Paul's day but not in today's changed society. This will not do, however, for he grounds it on a most basic Old Testament Scripture, to be found in Genesis 2 and 3.

How then are we to apply it today? How rigorously would Paul have applied it?

Would he have forbidden a woman to read the Scriptures in a service, or at least get a man to choose the portion? Would he even have excised from the hymn books the poetry of Fanny Crosby or Frances Ridley Havergal lest in their use in the church these women, though dead, may yet teach men in worship?

On the other hand, how would he view team ministries in which women fulfil many functions, including preaching and teaching, as members of the pastoral team, but under the overall leadership of a man? Would this fulfil the basic principle to be found in his teaching here?

We cannot pretend to know for sure. He is now in heaven and we are still on earth! His reference to women praying and prophesying in public (1 Cor. 11:5, 13), however, suggests moderate rather than rigorous application.

It is clear though that we must take this Scripture seriously and yet apply it sensitively. Faithfulness and merciful compassion were the two great characteristics of our Lord's own ministry (see especially Hebrews 2:17), and they must always be ours. We are not at liberty to set God's word aside but neither should we apply it harshly and insensitively.

Have most churches today grappled yet with the issue in these terms?

His teaching about qualifications for church office (1 Tim. 3) is full of challenge. The church needs leaders who will care for the flock and deal with its business. He lays emphasis on moral and spiritual qualities, and focuses especially on self-control, financial integrity and proper management of family life.

Such qualities are vital in every age and every culture.

Ordering the church in Crete

We have just one short letter to Titus, who was working in Crete, but it is a gem, with three passages (1:1-3, 2:11-14, 3:4-8) that together provide a wonderfully rich summary of the gospel.

There is much practical teaching here about church life, much of it covering the same kind of ground as 1 Timothy, and also material on the Christian's relationships, rather like Ephesians 5:21-6:9, Colossians 3:18-4:1 and Romans 13:1-7.

The issue of women teaching finds mention here also, but entirely in positive terms, for Paul says that older women should teach what is good, and train the younger women in the Christian lifestyle (Titus 2:3-5).

Whatever we may think of the way his teaching in 1 Timothy 2:11-15 should be applied today, there can be no doubt as to the enormous need for good teaching to be given to women and children. Judging by the proportions of men and women in the average modern church, with women usually very much in the majority, this role for Christian women is a considerable one.

We should notice what Paul has to say about foolish

controversies (3:9-11) as we have not commented on the similar teaching in 1 Timothy 1:3-7; 6:4,20, 21 and 2 Timothy 2:14-16, 23.

There are echoes here of internal debates and dissension over issues that are not fully spelled out, although some were certainly about the Law. Paul warns both younger men against quarrels over words.

It is essential for churches to be Bible-based. It is also vital, however, that issues of interpretation be kept in proportion.

The gospel is all-important, but we can surely live in harmony with Christians with whom we have minor disagreements about doctrine or practice! A contentious, divisive spirit is not the product of God's grace. To make a minor point into a big issue has sometimes moved people away from central truth altogether so that serious heresy has been the result.

If Paul had been alive today, he may well have exhorted us to treat big issues as big and small as small. In fact, this is what he was saying to Timothy and Titus.

16

Recognizing Personal Weakness

His frank acceptance of it

How do you visualize the apostle Paul? Do you think of him as a man of indomitable courage, prepared at all costs to face unlimited privations and especially to confront his foes and persecutors without flinching? In other words, a man who knew nothing of fear?

If so, you are wrong.

When he reminds the Corinthians of his first arrival to preach the gospel of Christ in their city, he says, 'I came to you in weakness and fear, and with much trembling' (1 Cor. 2:3). That may seem to you to be more like a description of you than of Paul. If so, it is your image of Paul that is wrong. Brave he most certainly was, but it was bravery in spite of fear, in the face of fear.

Such bravery is much more commendable than if it had been the product of a fearless temperament. What is particularly important is that it was the product of God's grace. Paul and you may be very different, but, if you are a Christian, you are one with him in your access to the grace of God.

Both from Acts and from his epistles, we can see that life as an evangelist and church-planter was anything but easy for Paul. In 2 Corinthians 11, developing more fully much of what he had already said in chapter 6:4-10, he gives a fearsome catalogue of his sufferings.

Some but not all of this can be documented from the Acts of the Apostles. Of course Luke's history is highly selective and concentrates on the northward and westward movement of the gospel. Paul is important to the story told there, not so much in terms of his sufferings, but in terms of the work he did to promote the onward march of the gospel. For this reason, we cannot expect a full account of his sufferings.

After this long catalogue, Paul says to his readers, 'Who is weak and I do not feel weak?'

He has already said that the treasure of the gospel is contained in jars of clay (2 Cor. 4:7). The reference is to the small vessels on sale in every market for use as containers and some of them also as lamps.

These fragile vessels symbolize the frailty and weakness of the human messengers of the gospel (2 Cor. 4:7ff.), who are the recipients of the priceless treasure of the gospel and through whom the light of Christ is to shine out in a dark world.

Paul declares too that, as a mortal man, he is like a tent-dweller awaiting the permanent dwelling of his resurrection body. Then he would enjoy glorious freedom from the weaknesses of this present life (2 Cor. 5:1-10).

One evidence of our weakness is of course illness. As we have seen, some take Paul's thorn in the flesh (2 Cor. 12:7) to have been an illness or other physical infirmity, while others dispute this.

We are on much safer ground in Galatians 4:13-15. Here he says that it was through illness he first brought the gospel to them. Perhaps, as many have thought, he contracted malaria when visiting the south coast of Asia Minor during his first missionary journey and so moved inland to the Galatian region (Acts 13:13,14).

It is possible too that he had eye-trouble, for he says that the Galatians would have been prepared, if possible, to give him their eyes, and he draws attention to his large handwriting (Gal. 6:11). If he had this kind of infirmity to contend with, this would underline for him still more the fact of his human weakness.

His recognition of a spiritual principle in it

There is no doubt at all but that Paul felt his weakness deeply. As he opens his heart to the Corinthians in his second letter to them, he stresses this. Time and again he refers to it.

What is so striking is that he is writing to a church which contained people who were critical of him.

In writing to them, we might have expected him to emphasise his strengths, his total fitness for the ministry God had given him to do. This is certainly what many of us would have been tempted to do.

It may be that Paul was tempted to do this also. Instead, he exposes to them his awareness of his weakness and need. Doesn't this show the completeness with which true Christian thinking cuts across that of the world?

Now it is good to see this, for a sense of weakness afflicts most of us from time to time, whether we admit it or not. Many of God's servants in the Bible show this in their own lives. We see it in Moses, aware of his lack of eloquence; in Gideon, facing his impotence in the face of the might of the Midianites; in Jeremiah, called as a young man to the daunting task of preaching to a rebellious nation.

What is even more astounding is the fact that Paul says that Christ too was weak! What? The Son of God? The Creator of the universe? The mighty Conqueror of Satan?

The Lord both of life and death? Yes, weak!

This shows how thoroughly Paul had grasped the true humanity of the Man of Nazareth. Jesus was crucified in weakness (2 Cor. 13:4).

This strongly suggests then that, in Paul's mind, weakness was not simply a physical thing. It included within itself an element of submissiveness. The woman, described by Peter as the weaker sex (1 Pet. 3:7) reveals this not simply at the muscular level but in her submissiveness (see 1 Pet. 3:6).

Paradoxically that weakness is really disguised strength. There is strength of character in the willingness to submit to another.

So it was in the case of Christ.

There is no doubt that the 'weakness' of Jesus in surrendering to those who had made themselves his enemies and persecutors, in allowing himself to submit to trials which were mockeries of justice, and finally to let himself be nailed to the tree, was immense strength in disguise. What spiritual strength he possessed to go through with this fearful programme of humiliation, shame, agony and unmitigated horror!

What mattered of course was Paul's willingness actively to face the sufferings that came his way.

The modern existentialist philosophers (especially Martin Heidegger) and existentialist theologians (like Rudolf Bultmann), have emphasised the importance of authentic as opposed to inauthentic existence.

What is inauthentic existence? It is the approach to life of those who are prepared simply to allow its events to happen to them. It is to have a largely passive existence in which your most significant actions are really simply reactions to circumstances that come to you unbidden and unplanned.

What then is authentic existence? This is life faced actively. It is decisive; it is positive.

Heidegger emphasised that, for authentic existence, the most important thing of all is to face death, to square up to it long before it comes.

Now we may have many reservations about Heidegger's philosophy and find other aspects of Bultmann's theology quite unacceptable, but this emphasis on facing and accepting death before it comes is biblical.

It was of course supremely true for Jesus.

Very early in his ministry he showed his awareness of the destiny of death which awaited him. On his final journey to Jerusalem he constantly spoke of it, and it is clear that he believed it would take place within the capital city itself. Yet, despite this, he kept his face steadfastly towards that city as his goal.

Now there have been some Christians so committed to martyrdom that it has become almost a death-wish, so much so that we get the feeling they would have been disappointed if it had not taken place. Ignatius of Antioch is sometimes quoted as a second-century example of this.

There was however nothing of this in the attitude of our Lord. Gethsemane shows us that he anticipated his forthcoming death with horror. Yet, despite this, he embraced it as the will of God. He took the cup of suffering and drank it to the dregs.

What about Paul? He says, 'I die every day' (1 Cor. 15:31). What does he mean?

In this passage, he undoubtedly has in mind the threat of physical death that was there all the time because of the opposition he constantly encountered. In this sense he embraced death at least as a daily possibility because it accorded with the vocation he had chosen, or, rather, the vocation for which God had chosen him.

Yet there is a deeper sense in which he embraced it. We have already seen that, for Paul, death and resurrection are not only the centre of the Christian gospel but also of the Christian life.

Paul did not simply teach this as a doctrine, but he lived it as a daily experience. He was able to say, 'I have been crucified with Christ and I no longer live,' although he could also go on to assert, 'but Christ lives in me' (Gal. 2:20). This is not simply a vivid statement of a doctrine, although it is this, but a personal confession of a life-attitude translated into a lifestyle.

Now human weakness finds its final confirmation in death. When death comes in old age or as a result of illness, it is often preceded by increasing bodily weakness.

A man who has thoroughly accepted the fact of death before the time has also, in that acceptance, come to terms with weakness. Thus we may understand the outlook of Paul.

This presents us with a challenge. How realistically have we faced our own weakness, even our own death? If facing these was a vital spiritual principle for him, it can be nothing less for us.

The thorn in Paul's flesh
There is one passage deservedly famous for its confession of weakness and also for its affirmation of the all-sufficiency of the grace of God. This is to be found in 2 Corinthians 12.

Here Paul says, 'To keep me from becoming conceited

because of these surpassingly great revelations, there was given me a thorn in my flesh, a messenger of Satan, to torment me. Three times I pleaded with the Lord to take it away from me.'

What was Paul's thorn in the flesh? This has been much discussed [1]. The majority view is that it was some kind of sickness or incapacity, some physical weakness from which he longed to be set free.

Paul does not himself give us a clear indication of its nature. This may have been quite deliberate on his part.

He may not have wanted to fasten attention on it, but rather to stress to his readers that it underlined his weakness and his need of the Divine grace which he then goes on to describe.

Perhaps then we need not be too concerned as to what it was. Was it a physical weakness, perhaps epilepsy or some kind of eye trouble? Both of these have been suggested. To the present writer, however, it seems less likely to have been this than either a temptation or some kind of human opposition.

It is a good principle of Biblical interpretation to look first of all in the Old Testament to find a clue to the meaning of a difficult New Testament passage. Often our perplexity with a New Testament passage is due to the fact that we simply do not know the Old Testament well enough.

In Numbers 33:55, Moses tells the Israelites that if they did not drive out the inhabitants of the land of Canaan, they would become 'barbs in your eyes and thorns in your sides'.

If Paul's words are an allusion to this passage, we could understand the reference either in terms of a temptation that would not go away or of human opponents causing trouble to him, and more probably the latter.

We will need to look at this passage again in the next two chapters.

His plea for prayer support

Paul wrote many letters. The ones we possess are probably only a fraction of those he penned. In several of those we possess, we find him asking for the prayers of his fellow-Christians.

We will look at these passages in a later chapter, where we will be concerned especially about the kind of things for which Paul asked prayer. Meantime though we ought to note that these requests underline his deep sense of weakness. In no way did he feel he was able to go it alone in his Christian work.

Why did he ask for prayer? Because he wanted to stress the inter-dependence of Christians? Because he believed that the church is a body and that, because of this, one part needs the ministry that other parts can give to it?

No doubt this was part of his thinking, but we should not imagine it to be his main motive. We can be sure he had a genuine need for prayer help.

We can see this particularly clearly in the prayer request we find in his letter to the Ephesians. In chapter 6:19, 20, he twice refers to his need to proclaim the gospel fearlessly. No doubt then he had the same fears many of us experience in our witness for Christ.

He had a strong and articulate conviction that the resources of God's grace are available to those who do his will, but he also knew that these resources are actually channelled to God's people in answer to prayer.

Some pastors and other Christian workers may give those for whom they have pastoral responsibility the impression, either that they are immune from temptation or that they have enormous spiritual strength. Their people may think they face every situation with complete confidence. It is not unknown for this to induce a most uneasy conscience in some of their people, who ask themselves why they do not have the same confidence themselves.

Paul's example certainly would not encourage any of us to practice this kind of concealment, for this is really what it is. Whatever we may appear to be, we are subject to many temptations and are utterly weak in ourselves.

Many of the folk to whom he was writing were in fact his converts. Because it had been his privilege to lead them to Christ, there is mutual love and he opens his heart to them completely. He tells them his inmost feelings, his hopes and his fears.

In this way, a deep dimension was added to the relationship he had with these Christians, many of whom were much newer in the faith than he was, and most, if not all of whom, will have had much less grasp of Christian truth than he had.

When we ask others to pray for us, we are acting as encouragers. We are really showing them the true spiritual value of their ministry to us.

Ministry should never be thought of as operating only in one direction. If one Christian preaches and another prays for him while he does so, who can say which of them has the greater ministry for Christ?

References

1. For a survey of the main views and arguments, see P. E. Hughes. *op.cit ad loc.*

17

Understanding Satan's Devices

This world is the arena of spiritual conflict.

The existence of a spiritual realm is much more widely recognized today than it was earlier this century. Many people are disenchanted with the materialistic and mechanistic view of the universe which used to prevail in western society and to which Christianity was the chief exception. It has proved spiritually unsatisfying and, for some, even intellectually inadequate.

Have such people been returning to the churches? In some cases, the answer is 'Yes!' There has however been another major factor in the situation. For several decades now eastern forms of mysticism, interest in the occult and even resurgent paganism have been growing in their influence on the general climate of thought in the west.

At one time the very idea of a powerful personal devil would have been dismissed with scorn. Today, as we know, there are groups of people who not only believe in his existence; they worship him.

Paul was well aware of the fact that he was involved in spiritual warfare.

His experience in serving the Lord Jesus and preaching his gospel was a mixed one. The joys were great but so were the sorrows. He saw people's lives gloriously transformed and fine churches established. He also encountered bitter opposition from unbelievers and there were even professing Christians who tried to undermine his work.

He rejoiced in the work of God; he also recognized the work of Satan.

Ruling human society

In Ephesians 6:10-20, he has much to say about the spiritual conflict.

In this passage, he recognizes that there are beings in the spiritual world antagonistic to the purposes of God. He says that our struggle is 'against the rulers, against the authorities, against the powers of this dark world and against the spiritual forces of evil in the heavenly realms' (Eph. 6:12).

His use of these various terms suggests that he saw some diversity among these beings. It is noticeable though that they all suggest authority and power. Let us not be under any misapprehension; the kingdom of evil is powerful, and it operates in 'this dark world'.

Paul was conscious in particular of the activities of 'the ruler of the kingdom of the air,' 'the devil,' 'the evil one' (Eph. 2:2; 6:11,16).

Unbelievers follow the ways of this world and of the ruler of the kingdom of the air. This unusual expression is presumably a reference to the fact that Satan has forces that belong to the spiritual realm under his control. He is at work in the disobedient, who follow the pattern of rebellion against God first set in the human race by Adam and Eve.

In another passage, Paul refers to the Lord's servant, and says, 'Those who oppose him he must gently instruct, in the hope that God will grant them repentance leading them to a knowledge of the truth, and that they will come to their senses and escape from the trap of the devil, who has taken them captive to do his will' (2 Tim. 2:25, 26).

No doubt most of Satan's dupes consider themselves to be free, but Paul makes it clear here that in fact they have been trapped by him for his own purposes.

It is very important to note that the responsibility is not all Satan's. People themselves need to recognize the wrong of their rebellion against God and turn away from their sins. In other words, the proclamation of the gospel, with its call for repentance, is vital.

So then, this means that prayer warfare and gospel preaching must go hand in hand. Remember that at one important stage in the church's life, the apostles said, 'we will give our attention to prayer and the ministry of the word' (Acts 6:4). The two should never be separated.

Opposing the gospel

When the gospel is preached, Satan is active.

What is he doing? He is blinding the minds of unbelievers so that they cannot see the glorious light of Christ's gospel (2 Cor. 4:3,4). This passage sounds the same note as our Lord's parable of the Sower in which he spoke of the devil coming and taking away the seed that had been sown (Mark 4:15).

Such things were true to Paul's experience. Acts records many occasions when he preached the gospel, doubtless with great clarity, and yet his message was rejected, sometimes with scorn. Why was this?

It was because of the activity of Satan. Satan's way is the way of darkness. He is a master of deceit.

This is evident in his first attack on humanity, recorded in Genesis 3. He presented disobedience as the key to knowledge and higher status, whereas in fact it opened the door to misery.

As we read on in the Book of Genesis, we find that the sin of deceit, which began the story of human rebellion against God, became the leading sin of the continuing story there, even amongst the people of God. Abraham, Isaac, Jacob and his sons were all guilty of it. No wonder Paul wrote of 'the devil's schemes' (Eph. 6:11)!

What does he mean when he describes the devil as 'the god of this age' (2 Cor. 4:4)? Is it the power of Satan he has in view? Probably there is something else. Remember that a god is an object of worship.

Human beings worship a great many objects that are unworthy of their worship, but in fact there is only one God, the great God and Father of our Lord Jesus Christ, the Lord of creation, of history and of salvation. If other gods do not exist, does this mean that the worship accorded to them therefore has no significance at all?.

This was not Paul's view. He says, 'the sacrifices of pagans are offered to demons, not to God' (1 Cor. 10:20; cf. Deut. 32:16,17). This worship is received in the spiritual realm, but not by divine beings.

So, when Paul describes Satan as the 'god of this age,' he is probably thinking along these lines. People worshipping false gods are kept in their blindness by Satan himself, the ultimate object of that worship, the monarch of the whole kingdom of evil.

We too need to recognize this dimension in Christian work. This idea is unlikely to be popular these days, when many people are becoming more and more aware of the diversity of religious belief in the world. If however we are to be faithful to the word of God, we need to accept its teaching at this point as at all others.

It does not mean we should be harsh in our attitude to

people of other religions. Far from it. Christians should be the most loving and caring of people, good neighbours going out of their way to help others. In fact, our love will lack a most important dimension unless we recognize their greatest need to be liberation from Satan's bondage.

Fathering heresies

What is the worst form of darkness? It is darkness disguised as light. Such 'light' is a deceptive masterpiece of Satan.

Analyse the teaching of any system of religion or substitute for religion which has held multitudes of people in its grip and you will find it to be an amalgam of truth and error. The element of truth is Satan's bait, but look out for the hook!

Paul saw darkness disguised as light in the presence of heresies within the churches or in the areas where they were situated.

In writing to the church at Rome, he warns them against 'those who cause divisions and put obstacles in your way that are contrary to the teaching you have learned ... By smooth talk and flattery they deceive the minds of naive people' (Rom. 16:17,18).

His strong reassurance to the church that 'the God of peace will soon crush Satan under your feet', follows this warning (Rom. 16:20).

This shows, as clearly as possible, that he did not think Satan's activity was restricted to the attempt to retain human beings in his control. He knew that the devil was also at work within local churches.

In 2 Corinthians 11, he writes about those at Corinth who professed to be apostles. He does not in fact accuse them of promoting false teaching, but, of course, arrogant assertion of special status in the church has often been associated with false teaching or has eventually led to it.

He regards them as agents of Satan, and does not hesitate to say so. He declares, 'For such men are false apostles, deceitful workmen, masquerading as apostles of Christ. And no wonder, for Satan himself masquerades as an angel of light. It is not surprising, then, if his servants masquerade as servants of righteousness. Their end will be what their actions deserve' (2 Cor. 11:13-15).

Fostering pride

God and Satan only have one thing in common: their desire that others should be conformed to their own characters. Paul certainly saw this as a mark of the work of Satan.

Writing to Timothy, he counsels against the appointment of a new convert to the office and work of an overseer in the church, lest he become conceited and so, manifesting Satanic pride, find himself under a similar judgement. An overseer needs a good reputation in the community or he may fall into disgrace and so into the devil's trap (1 Tim. 3:6,7).

Satan no doubt laughs when he has professed servants of Christ doing his will and walking in his ways. Pride in a servant of Christ may not get him on to the front page of a national newspaper in the way some other sins will, but it can do immense damage to the local testimony of his church.

Satan is sure too to be glad when he sees a new convert, with a somewhat dramatic conversion story, constantly pushed into the limelight, and beginning to enjoy it. None of us did God a favour by being converted!

The evil one wants to disturb the peace of the church and

to encourage antagonism between its members. So often this can be traced to pride.

At Corinth the parties were associated with the names of leaders who were not then physically present in the church. We can be sure though that the real party-leaders were not these people but folk on the spot.

Each of these local leaders probably got some sort of 'buzz' from promoting his party. Without doubt, pride would be the cause of this party spirit and pride would keep it going.

Pride takes many forms. When I am angry at some supposed slight, the real problem is my own self-regarding spirit. Why do I always reckon my anger with you to be righteous but yours with me unrighteous? There is in fact a thin line between righteous and unrighteous anger and so, in Ephesians 4:27, Paul warns his readers against giving the devil a foothold in this way.

What is the most frequent cause of the destruction of a flourishing local church? Without a shadow of doubt, it is pride.

Hindering the work
What part did Satan play in Paul's own experience?

In 1 Thessalonians 2:17, 18, he says, 'But, brothers, when we were torn away from you for a short time (in person, not in thought), out of our intense longing we made every effort to see you. For we wanted to come to you - certainly I, Paul, did, again and again - but Satan stopped us.'

Now this is a striking and unexpected comment from a man who had such a sense of the Divine sovereignty and of God's commission in his own life. Does this mean that Satan could actually hinder the work of God through such a man as he was?

If Satan could hinder Paul, what hope is there for the rest of us in our ministries?

We need to ask what form this hindering took?

Was it the pressure of other missionary activity on Paul's part? Surely not, for it was God's purpose that the gospel should be preached far and wide. Was it then some personal problem, perhaps an illness? If so, we have no real means of telling, for neither the Thessalonian epistles nor the account Luke gives of this period of Paul's ministry give us any clue to such a cause.

So this leaves the possibility that it is a reference to opposition from human sources.

We know there was trouble from the Jews and also from the secular authorities (Acts 17:5-10; cf. 1 Thess. 1:6; 2:2,14). Paul was very much aware of the fact that Satan often finds human agents to do his work. It seems then altogether likely he has these in mind.

Is he commenting here on the terms of the bail imposed by the magistrates on Jason and his friends? We cannot be sure, but it seems very likely. It was probably a condition of it that Paul was not to return to the area, at least within the term of office of the magistrates who made the ruling. He apparently had no problems in sending Timothy (1 Thess. 3:1-10). The terms of the bail probably did not include him.

Should Jason and his friends have gone along with the city officials here? Perhaps they should have stood their ground and endeavoured to show that all the talk about a rival king was based on a distortion of the Christian message (Acts 17:6,7). It was no evidence then of a seditious spirit. We need though to remember that, as new Christians, this would have been more difficult for them than it would have been for Paul and Silas. We should not misunderstand Paul when, in the Ephesian letter, he says that our struggle is not against flesh and blood. He certainly does not mean to imply that human beings have no part in the opposition.

Rather his point is that our chief adversaries are in the spiritual realm. Those who oppose the work of the Lord on the human level should be seen as agents of evil spiritual forces.

Since he exhorts his readers to put on the spiritual armour and to take hold of the spiritual weapons provided by God (Eph. 6:10-20), we might be inclined to ask why these weapons were not available to him in his desire to get back to Thessalonica?

This would be to forget that in fact he was successful in his main concern, which was to reassure himself about his converts there. He did this by sending one of his missionary colleagues instead of going himself. Undoubtedly he would have preferred to go himself, but this fulfilled his main purpose just as well.

Over-reaching himself

What is the relationship between the sovereign purpose of God and the activity of Satan? This question comes to the fore quite explicitly in Paul's 'thorn in the flesh' reference in 2 Corinthians 12. A study of this passage can be of great help to a Christian worker.

The first thing we notice is that Paul says it was given to him. He does not say so explicitly, but this suggests it originated from God. Yet it is 'a messenger of Satan'. How strange!

The mystery deepens when we consider not simply its origin but its purpose.

He says, first of all, that it was 'to keep me from

becoming conceited because of these surpassingly great revelations.' This certainly looks like a Divine purpose. Satan may have many aims, but keeping God's servants humble is not one of them! After all, he had fostered pride in the hearts of the false apostles, as Paul has indicated in the previous chapter of this very letter.

Yet the apostle also says its purpose was to torment him. Now, without doubt, this is Satanic. God may discipline his workers, but he never torments them.

It looks then as if it was a situation in which both God and Satan had purposes. There are many situations like that.

There is an outstanding example of this in the experience of the Lord Jesus Christ. Matthew tells us that, after his baptism 'Jesus was led by the Spirit into the desert to be tempted by the devil' (Matt. 4:1). Mark and Luke say much the same thing.

Even Satanic temptation is not outside the purpose of God. He is able to bring good out of evil, in a way no other can do. Temptation resisted in the power of the Spirit strengthens character.

What then is the right attitude of the Christian in such circumstances? Paul tells us what he did. In fact, although he does not make this explicit, he followed the example of Christ in Gethsemane, for he pleaded with the Lord three times for this thorn to be removed from his flesh.

Perhaps this suggests some parallel between what was a cup for Christ and what was a thorn for Paul.

Certainly there were differences. In Christ's case it was something in prospect which he needed to accept and drink voluntarily. In Paul's case it was part of his experience already.

The parallel then must have been the element of suffering involved in it, although we should not forget that this was much less intense for Paul than it was for his Saviour. There were thorns for Jesus too, in the cruel crown pressed on his head, but the pain from them would not compare with that of the nails. In fact, the spiritual sufferings of Jesus were much greater even than his many-sided physical sufferings.

It is not normal of course for human beings to welcome suffering as a good thing in itself. In fact, when this does happen it would suggest a diseased and not a healthy mind. Christ certainly did not embrace suffering as a good, considered purely in itself, but rather his human spirit shrank from it and he asked three times for it to be removed.

So Paul recognised two different purposes in what had happened to him, a Divine and a Satanic purpose.

An experience of trial, of temptation or of suffering, can have different effects on two different people. The same fire that hardens the egg also softens the butter. Trial may refine or it may coarsen us. Our attitude to it is all-important.

Paul took it to the Lord in prayer. He told him of his longing to be rid of this thorn. Not once but three times he brought his request. Instead of its removal, he was given a deeper experience of the grace of God through this.

How Satan had over-reached himself! He set out to thwart God's purposes in Paul's life, but God had such control of the total situation that Paul was kept humble and discovered in a profound way how powerful God's grace was.

Satan certainly did not want that!

Defeated by God's power
Resistance to Satan is an element in authentic Christian living, for we are to resist temptation in Christ's name.

When however there are circumstances that Satan is using, our recourse is to God. He can change the circumstances or give us grace to endure whatever suffering arises from them for us.

The great passage in Ephesians 6 shows Paul's total confidence in God. Before he ever refers to the evil spiritual forces, he says, 'Be strong in the Lord and in his mighty power. Put on the full armour of God' (Eph. 6:10,11). He recognizes the power of the enemy forces, but he sees them always in the context of God's mighty power.

The spiritual armour is provided in Christ, but it must be put on by faith. Paul's language here is realistic and should warn us against complacency as well as inspiring our confidence in God.

Some commentators take the items of armour here to be objective. In other words, they represent what Christ is to us. He is the Truth, and he is our Righteousness and our Salvation. We are therefore to find safety in him for the whole of our being.

Others take them to be subjective, and to represent what we actually become, as God's Spirit reproduces the likeness of Christ in us. We are to be truthful and righteous and to enjoy in our experience the fullness of salvation.

Do we need to choose between these two interpretations, when Paul's language is rich enough to include both? Perhaps not.

The shield of faith surely combines the two, for objectively Christ is our Shield but we are to trust in him in actual experience. What we can certainly say is that our commitment to Christ as the Truth only evidences itself as real when we become truthful ourselves, and this is true of the other items too.

The shoes show that we are to advance into enemy territory with the gospel, while the sword indicates that God's word is our weapon both for offence and defence.

Some of us, who are not a standard size, find it difficult to buy clothes 'off the peg'. What a blessing then to realize that the spiritual armour God provides is a perfect fit for us all!

You may feel that you are part of a small detachment, cut off from the main army, or even a completely isolated soldier. This is rarely the case. Don't forget Elijah and the seven thousand who had not bowed the knee to Baal (1 Kings 19:13-18)!

Even if it is true, however, the lines of communication are always open. God has given us the great resource of prayer. In prayer, we can be constantly in touch with and dependent on our heavenly Captain. His power is infinite and, through his death, resurrection and ascension, he is seated in the place of absolute power, far above all (Eph. 1:19-21).

Thanks be to God!

18

Looking to the Lord

He recognized its importance

As we read Paul's letters, we become aware of his deep sense of weakness. We also see that he knew he faced the opposition of a great enemy. Put the two together and you would seem to have a prescription for disaster.

In fact, if you look at the situation of a Christian believer - any believer in any place at any time - you may think his chances of success as a servant of God to be nil.

The whole thing seems ludicrous. We see this if we try to illustrate it. Someone trying to construct a dam across the mouth of the Amazon single-handed; a man attempting to build a house at the height of a hurricane; somebody trying to climb Everest on crutches. Take your pick. You will never find anything more ridiculous than a feeble sinner trying to worst Satan.

There must have been times when it seemed like that to Paul. After all, he did not live a cloistered life. He was out there facing the great enemy every day and never able to escape from this feeling of powerlessness.

In his Second Letter to the Corinthians, he was writing about the awesome demands of Christian service. He interjected, 'And who is equal to such a task?' (2:16).

The only possible answer is, of course, 'Nobody!'

Preaching has been described as 'twenty minutes to raise the dead'. Raising the dead is not exactly commonplace! You could not do it in twenty life-times, let alone twenty minutes.

Yet Paul went on serving the Lord; he went on preaching. Why?

Because he knew that one person with God is in a majority. A few verses later on in that same letter, he says, 'Not that we are competent in ourselves to claim anything for ourselves, but our competence comes from God. He has made us competent as ministers of a new covenant - not of the letter but of the Spirit; for the letter kills, but the Spirit gives life' (2 Cor. 3:5,6).

Paul was well aware of the fact that as a servant of God, he was an agent of the risen Christ, an instrument of the Holy Spirit. He had no power in himself, but he could be a channel of Divine power. Not only so, but God could complement and support his Spirit-empowered activity in so many different ways through his control of circumstances.

As a servant of Christ, there was no question of his work being done on the basis of his own resources or by his own unaided wisdom. He needed to keep in close touch with his Lord through prayer.

This is something every Christian worker needs to remember. God may have bestowed gifts of ministry, insight into Scripture, preaching skills. If he has done this for you, you are privileged. These will accomplish nothing, however, unless all the work is done in prayerful dependence on God.

Paul has a great deal to say about prayer in his letters.[1] In fact, there is no letter we have from him that does not contain at least one reference to it, except the brief letter to Titus.

The keen student of Paul's letters might ask, 'What about Galatians?'

It is true that the usual terminology of prayer is not employed there, but there is one passage in which we can see, not only that he prayed, but that his prayer-life was both deep and costly. He addresses them as 'My dear children, for whom I am again in the pains of childbirth until Christ is formed in you' (Gal. 4:19).

Paul did not mean simply that he was very worried about them, and that his nights were sleepless because of the pain he felt. A man of God takes all his worries, about others as well as about himself, to God in prayer.

There is little doubt that we could construct a whole theology of prayer from what he writes. Moreover we find in his letters a powerful example and challenge for our own praying.

He prayed for his friends - broadly

How did Paul minister to the infant churches God had enabled him to found? He did this in at least three ways: he visited them himself, he encouraged others to visit them and he wrote them letters.

No doubt all this was indispensable. It is important though to remember that he had another vital ministry to them, and that was the ministry of intercessory prayer.

We can understand his special interest and prayer concern for the churches which had come into being as a result of his own evangelistic work. After he had left a town, with people who had responded to Christ gathered into a church, he would of course give them the support through prayer that he could no longer give them in terms of his physical presence.

It is much more of a surprise to find him writing to the Roman church and saying, 'God, whom I serve with my whole heart in preaching the gospel of his Son, is my witness how constantly I remember you in my prayers at all times' (Rom. 1:9,10).

This church was not founded by him. He had never visited it, although he was hoping to put that right, and no doubt was praying as part of his preparation for the visit.

Also, of course, as we see in chapter 16 of his letter to them, many people there were known to him. So no doubt much of his prayer for this church would focus on the needs of particular individuals.

There may well however have been another reason.

If all roads led to Rome, it was equally true that they all led from it. It could be a most strategic centre for the spread of the gospel in many directions. No doubt his realization of this would affect his prayers for the believers there.

Many of Paul's letters to churches start with his expression of thanksgiving to God for the readers. In close connection with this, he often tells them that he prays regularly for them. This must have been a great encouragement to them.

He knew that these companies of Christian people had been brought into being by the Lord so that they might bear witness to him. They were to spread the good news of God's love in Christ to many others.

He prayed for his friends - individually
He prayed not only for churches, but for individuals.

In the very last letter we have from him, we can see this. He tells Timothy that he prays for him constantly: 'night and day I constantly remember you in my prayers' (2 Tim. 1:3).

Timothy was a close colleague. He had laboured with him as a member of his travelling evangelistic team. He had also gone to Ephesus with a very specific commission, and the work he was doing there was really an extension of Paul's own.

Paul seems to have worked with Philemon in some way, and he prays too for him (Philemon 1-7). His evangelistic concern comes out clearly when he says, 'I pray that you may be active in sharing your faith.'

From the evidence we have in his letters, Paul must have had a large prayer list. He was not content simply to lead people to Christ and to give them instruction and encouragement. He shouldered the responsibility of continued prayer remembrance for them.

Many other great men and women of God can teach us this same lesson. Robert Murray McCheyne, for instance, used to move from seat to seat in his church in Dundee. At each of the seats he would pray for those who habitually occupied them. No wonder there was such blessing through his preaching!

He prayed for his friends - deeply

Paul's prayers for the churches are deep.

It was not that he was unconcerned about the more mundane aspects of their life. He must have been.

Fundamentally though he longed to see them growing in maturity and coming to possess all for which Christ had possessed them. We see this so clearly in his letter to the Colossian church.

Here, writing about Christ, he says, 'We proclaim him, admonishing and teaching everyone with all wisdom, so that we may present everyone perfect in Christ. To this end I labour, struggling with all his energy, which so powerfully works in me' (Col. 1:28,29).

What was this labour? We may think of it simply in

terms of preaching and teaching, but it was certainly more than this.

It had a prayer dimension too, because in the very next verse (separated, unfortunately, by a chapter division), he says, 'I want you to know how much I am struggling for you and for those at Laodicea, and for all who have not met me personally.'

This struggling could have no physical reference, for they were separated by many miles. It must be his way of saying that he was engaging in spiritual warfare on their behalf.

He prayed for the spiritual advancement of his readers, both at the level of understanding and at the level of doing. This comes out in prayer after prayer.

Writing, for instance, to the Philippians, he says, 'And this is my prayer: that your love may abound more and more in knowledge and depth of insight, so that you may be able to discern what is best and may be pure and blameless until the day of Christ, filled with the fruit of righteousness that comes through Jesus Christ - to the glory and praise of God' (Phil. 1:9-11).

Again, writing to the Colossians, he says, 'We have not stopped praying for you and asking God to fill you with the knowledge of his will through all spiritual wisdom and understanding. And we pray this in order that you may live a life worthy of the Lord and may please him in every way' (Col. 1:9,10).

Two great prayers are found in his letter to the Ephesians, at the close of chapters 1 and 3. In this letter, Paul often moves off at a tangent and then returns to his previous train of thought at the point at which he left it. It is therefore possible that, in the mind of the apostle, these were really two parts of the same prayer.

In fact, it is not at all certain where the first prayer ends. Does it go right through to the end of the chapter? If not, where are we to find its end?

Our difficulty in this regard is worth pondering. It really means that for Paul deep thinking and deep praying were closely related to each other. The wonderful truths about God in Christ resided not only in his mind but in his heart. They were profoundly theological and profoundly devotional at the same time.

It was said of David McIntyre, who for twenty-five years was principal of the Bible Training Institute (now the Glasgow Bible College), that there was often a very thin line between his ministry to others and the outpourings of his heart in prayer to God.

James Denney, the Scottish theologian, used to say that he had little interest in a theology that could not be preached. We may say too of Paul that he had little interest in a theology that could not be prayed.

In the first prayer, he prays for a much deeper understanding on the part of the Christians to whom he writes. In the second, he prays for a deepened experience.

Understanding and experience are of course often related to each other as cause and effect. Paul knew however that deeper understanding, although making deeper experience possible, does not lead to it inevitably. He therefore prays for this also.

Without doubt his gospel orientation will have determined the nature of his prayers for the churches. He wanted to see them becoming strong in the Lord and attractively Christ-like so that their testimony would be God-honouring and evangelistically effective.

There is no doubt that in his praying he would be

occupied with elements of immaturity in the churches. He was deeply concerned about such things and, as a true man of God, Paul turned his deepest concerns into prayer.

What would he bring to God? The tendencies to division at Rome, the much deeper tendency in the same direction at Corinth, the trouble between Euodia and Syntyche at Philippi, the influence of the heretics at Colosse, the deeply troubling consequences of the teaching of the Judaizers at Galatia.

It is well worth noting though that he often gives thanks for the churches to whom he writes. They may not have consisted of perfect Christians, but their members were people who trusted in Christ and they were showing evidence of the reality of that faith in love to others. For this he gave thanks.

He asked his friends to pray for him

Paul had a strong sense of the unity in variety to be found in the church of Christ.

His analogy of the body, expressed in some detail in 1 Corinthians 12, was used to teach several lessons. One of these was the variety of gifts God has given his people and the need for each Christian to exercise these for the benefit of all.

There is, however, no suggestion whatever that prayer is one of these individual gifts and therefore that only certain members of the church were called to minister in prayer. It was rather to be a function of the whole fellowship.

In the final chapter of his letter to the Ephesians he calls on his readers to engage in spiritual warfare in the power of God, and clothed in the armour he has provided. He then goes on to call them to prayer. This was meant to be a challenge to them all.

It is noteworthy that he encourages them to pray very broadly, but also very specifically and with individual reference.

'Keep on praying for all the saints. Pray also for me' (Eph. 6:18,19). Between the two poles of 'all the saints' and 'me' our prayer life is to range. It is good to remember God's work in many parts of the world, but we also have very specific prayer responsibilities too.

For what does he ask prayer?

As we seek an answer to this question, we become very much aware of that gospel-centredness we have seen so often in other ways.

In his First Letter to the Thessalonians, he simply asks them to pray for him and his companions (1 Thess. 5:25), but in the Second he asks them to 'pray for us that the message of the Lord may spread rapidly and be honoured, just as it was with you. And pray that we may be delivered from wicked and evil men' (2 Thess. 3:1,2).

This second request receives some illumination when we consider his prayer request to the Roman Christians.

He says, 'I urge you, brothers, by our Lord Jesus Christ and by the love of the Spirit, to join me in my struggle by praying to God for me. Pray that I may be rescued from the unbelievers in Judea and that my service in Jerusalem may be acceptable to the saints there, so that by God's will I may come to you with joy and together with you be refreshed' (Rom. 15:30-32).

He had already told them that his plan was to come to them so that he could 'preach the gospel also to you who are at Rome' (Rom 1:15). So we can see that his concern for rescue was not so much personal as due to a deep desire to be able to continue his preaching of the gospel and his ministry to those who had received it.

When he wrote to the Thessalonians and the Romans, he was very much the active missionary, going from place to place with the good news of Jesus. He remembered both the glad reception and also the opposition his message had encountered at Thessalonica. It is not at all surprising then that his prayer request to the Thessalonians should reflect these facts, which would not only be very much in his mind but also in the minds of the Thessalonian Christians.

When he wrote Ephesians and Colossians, however, he was in prison. What did he ask his readers to pray for? That he might be given better conditions of imprisonment? No, it is still the gospel that is his dominant concern.

In Ephesians he asks prayer, 'that whenever I open my mouth, words may be given me so that I will fearlessly make known the mystery of the gospel, for which I am an ambassador in chains. Pray that I may declare it fearlessly, as I should' (Eph. 6:19,20).

To the Colossians, he writes in similar fashion: 'And pray for us, too, that God may open a door for our message, so that we may proclaim the mystery of Christ, for which I am in chains. Pray that I may proclaim it clearly, as I should' (Col. 4:3,4).

He did say to Philemon, 'I hope to be restored to you in answer to your prayers' (Philemon 22). No doubt he longed to be out and about again to continue his work of evangelism outside the limits imposed by his imprisonment.

Although we do find these particular requests for prayer, he is not always quite as specific. In writing his first letter to the Thessalonians, he says, very simply and touchingly, 'Brothers, pray for us' (1 Thess. 5:25).

So we see that the great apostle had no sense of lordly

independence from the churches he was largely instrumental in bringing into being. Now that they were Christians themselves they had access to the throne of grace in prayer. They could remember him and support him with fervent prayer as he continued to go from place to place with the gospel.

This kind of fellowship is a privilege both for those who are prayed for and for those who pray. It is not easy to say which are the more blessed.

References

1. A useful study of each of these may be found in D. Coggan, *The Prayers of the New Testament*. n.p. 1967. pp. 87-167.

19

Experiencing God's Grace

Paul was well aware of the fact that he was unable to face his problems alone and that there was no need even to try to do so. Our study of his prayer-life should have made this very clear to us.

What then did he seek from God? It can all be summed up in the one word, 'grace'.

It is not always the case that the popular understanding of a word expresses its meaning accurately. You could not, however, get a better definition of grace than simply 'unmerited favour', which is what most Christians know about its meaning.

At times it may mean more than this, but it never means less.

It is important to give full value both to the noun and to the adjective in this definition.

As far as God is concerned, his favour towards us is complete. We are accepted into all the fullness of his love and blessing.

It has been easy for the author to write the two sentences of that last paragraph. No doubt they have been easy enough for the reader to read. To grasp all the implications of them and to know the full wonder of this acceptance is more than can be accomplished in one lifetime. Perhaps this is one of the purposes of heaven!

As far as we are concerned, our lack of merit is complete. We do not deserve his favour and we never have. More than that, we never will, for even when we are perfected in heaven, we will be eternally dependent on God's grace as far as our past sins are concerned.

It would not be too much to say that, for Paul, the whole Christian life in its every aspect, is the product of God's grace.

He experienced the grace of God in salvation

As we have seen, there has been much recent discussion of Romans 7 by modern scholars and many of them now consider that this chapter is not autobiographical.

However much Paul may or may not have been aware of deep spiritual need before he met Christ on the Damascus Road, we know that from that moment onwards, he was very much aware of his personal sin. Many of us know from experience that consciousness of sin can become much fuller and sharper once we have started on the Christian pathway.

Also this awareness of sin certainly included his life during the period that ended with his conversion as he viewed that retrospectively. He makes this abundantly clear in 1 Timothy 1:12-16.

Earlier in the chapter, he had given a list of sins against the law, including 'those who kill their fathers or mothers'. He goes on to describe himself as 'once a blasphemer and a persecutor and a violent man' and then calls himself the worst of sinners.

What, worse than those who murder their parents? Apparently, even though he had 'acted in ignorance and unbelief' (verse 13). This shows how seriously he viewed opposition to Christ and his gospel.

Twice in this passage he says that he was shown mercy and 'the grace of our Lord was poured out on me abundantly'. He never ceased to wonder at this.

In Romans 2 and 3, he emphasized that the Jew, just as much as the Gentile, was guilty before God and therefore in need of salvation. He was himself a Jew and therefore, of course, guilty.

When he quoted the Old Testament words, 'There is no-one righteous, not even one' (Rom. 3:10; 1 Kings 8:46), and when he went on to say, 'for all have sinned and fall short of the glory of God' (Rom. 3:23), he was obviously including himself.

We should notice also what he says in Galatians 2: 15, 16. Here he quotes a conversation in which he said to Peter, 'We who are Jews by birth and not "Gentile sinners" know that a man is not justified by observing the law, but by faith in Jesus Christ. So we, too, have put our faith in Christ Jesus that we may be justified by faith in Christ and not by observing the law, because by observing the law no-one will be justified.'

His personal retreat from self-justification is also mentioned in Philippians 3, where, after listing his former causes for religious pride as a Jew, he then declares, 'But whatever was to my profit I now consider loss for the sake of Christ' (verse 7).

The New Testament writers have a number of different ways of expounding the great salvation God has provided for sinners. For example, sometimes they think of it as deliverance, at others as cleansing, at others as being brought out of darkness into light, at others as being brought near to God. The gospel preacher has no excuse if he bores his listeners by proclaiming the gospel news of Jesus in much the same way every time!

It is well known, of course, that Paul uses the language of righteousness and of justification much more than any other writer, and that he gloried in the fact that, through Christ's atoning death, sinners may be declared righteous in the sight of God.

His love for the doctrine of justification must surely have been as a result of his personal experience and not simply because he gloried in it theologically. Facing the question of his personal relationship with God, which was of course, much in the mind of the average Jew, and especially in the mind of the Pharisaic Jew, at this time, he must have known that without Christ and his saving work he was forever lost.

He experienced the grace of God in service
Bible study can yield some surprises.

The writer well recalls a time when he was studying the words 'grace' and 'mercy' in the New Testament by the use of a concordance. He discovered to his amazement that Paul uses these words just as frequently about Christian service as he does in connection with salvation.

This is worth pondering.

How easy it is for a Christian simply to think of his service for Christ as a gift he is giving to his Saviour! It is true of course, that Paul could and sometimes did think of it that way.

Writing to the Romans, he says. 'I have written to you quite boldly on some points, as if to remind you of them again, because of the grace God gave me to be a minister of Christ Jesus to the Gentiles with the priestly duty of pro-claiming the gospel of God, so that the Gentiles might become an offering acceptable to God, sanctified by the Holy Spirit' (Rom. 15:15,16).

What does he mean? He is using the Old Testament language of priesthood and sacrifice, figuratively of course rather than literally. The sacrificial offering he was privileged to bring to God consisted of the Gentiles who had become Christians through his preaching ministry.

Even here, however, he wrote of God's grace in his ministry, which tunes in with his thought elsewhere, where he thinks of service as a gift bestowed on us by God. We do not and never will deserve this service. It is a great privilege, an evidence of God's grace to us.

Paul was particularly moved by the fact that his apostolic commission was given to him after he had been a foremost persecutor of the Christians.

Writing to the Corinthians, he says, 'For I am the least of the apostles and do not even deserve to be called an apostle, because I persecuted the church of God. But by the grace of God I am what I am, and his grace to me was not without effect. No, I worked harder than all of them - yet not I, but the grace of God that was with me' (1 Cor. 15:9,10).

He says again, 'I became a servant of this gospel by the gift of God's grace given me through the working of his power. Although I am less than the least of all God's people, this grace was given me: to preach to the Gentiles the unsearchable riches of Christ' (Eph. 3:7,8).

When he says that he did his hard work in the service of God by God's own grace, this reveals that he was aware of the need for constant dependence on him. Grace to him was now not only an attitude of God, it was an act of God. Because God accepted him in Christ, he empowered him in his service for Christ.

So it was not simply a matter of the appointment to high service of somebody who did not deserve this. Wonderful as that was, it was only half the story. The power of God was operative on his behalf throughout the whole course of his service. Not surprisingly, then, he calls this power 'grace' as well.

Christ had not simply appointed him and then left him to his own resources to carry out the terms of that appointment. The resources were his through the Holy Spirit, who is the Spirit of Christian service as well as of Christian salvation.

A small child was travelling by bus with his mother. Seated just ahead of them was a woman wearing a beautiful coat. 'What a lovely coat, Mummy!' said the boy. 'I am going to buy you a coat like that.' 'But,' said his mother, 'coats like that cost a lot of money. Where will you get the money?' That question caused him no problems! 'From you, of course,' he declared!

The gift of service we so long to render our Saviour may seem impossible, until we see what rich resources he has himself given us to make it possible.

He experienced the grace of God in sanctification

The word 'sanctification' refers of course to God's work of making us holy, of making us, in fact, like the Lord Jesus Christ. It is the Holy Spirit who does this.

We are called to holiness. Paul writes to the Thessalonians, 'It is God's will that you should be sanctified ... For God did not call us to be impure, but to live a holy life. Therefore, he who rejects this instruction does not reject man but God, who gives you his Holy Spirit' (1 Thess. 4:3,7,8).

The reference to the Holy Spirit here is important. The order of the Greek words in the sentence serves somewhat to underline the word 'holy'. The standard of Christian holiness is high, but Paul will not let his readers make this an excuse. He is reminding them that they are not left to their own resources but that God's Spirit has been given to them to enable them to be holy.

In Romans 7:14-25, as we have seen, Paul describes an inner struggle, either his own specifically or a common experience which he shared. Many commentators take this to be a description of the struggles of a Pharisee to keep the law, while many others believe it to refer to the moral struggle experienced by a Christian after his conversion.

Two facts stand out in the passage. One is the person's real desire to do God's will and the other is the constant repetition of the word 'I' with no reference to God until Christ is mentioned in verse 25. Those who take the passage as a description of a Christian stress the first fact, while those who deny this stress the second. Obviously any interpretation needs to take full account of both facts.

It seems best to view the passage as setting out the experience of a Christian man, but with the all-important fact of the Holy Spirit's gracious power abstracted from it. The man has a deep desire to please the Lord, but he is aware of the fact that, even as a Christian, he does not have adequate personal resources with which to do this. Every experience of inner conflict resulting in failure brings this home to us.

Then our resources in Christ made available through the Spirit are expounded in the following chapter. In this way we are taught that, just because we are unable even as Christians to do what we most want to do, to please the God who has saved us, we need to depend on the mighty power and grace of the Spirit to enable us to walk in God's way.

Paul sums it up so well in Galatians 5:16, where he says, '... live by the Spirit, and you will not gratify the desires of the sinful nature.' We Christians need to recognize our tendency to rely on our own resources and learn more and more to depend on God's grace through the Holy Spirit.

We need Romans 7 so that we may never forget our great weakness; we need Romans 8 to remind us constantly of the power of God's grace.

He experienced the grace of God in suffering
In considering the passage in 2 Corinthians 12 where Paul writes about his thorn in the flesh, we have seen that this was a sore trial to him.

Whatever this thorn was, Paul prayed three times for its removal.

Was this prayer answered? Yes it was, but not in the terms of his actual asking. God met his need although not along lines suggested by the actual terms of his prayer.

The Bible is in fact full of such experiences. The history of God's people since Bible times provides many further examples of it.

Think, for instance, of Abraham pleading with God for Sodom.

As we read the account of it in Genesis 18, we have no reason whatever to doubt his earnestness. This was very great, and he advanced more and more in his boldness as the prayer moved towards its close. Eventually, his request was that God would not destroy the city if he found ten righteous people there.

Did God hear Abraham's prayer? Of course, he did. In

fact, he said quite explicitly, 'For the sake of ten, I will not destroy it' (v. 32).

Yet Sodom was destroyed! It was so wicked that ten righteous people could not be found there.

That might suggest to us that, although of course God's faithfulness was not in doubt in any way, in the actual event itself there was no positive answer to Abraham's agonized prayer. Abraham wanted to see Sodom saved. His ever-progressing prayer stopped too soon, so that the longing of his heart was in vain.

If however we were to come to that conclusion, we would be wrong, utterly wrong.

Even in the event itself, God did answer Abraham's prayer, although not in the terms in which he put that prayer to him. The longing in his heart was fully met.

There can be no real doubt that the great burden of Abraham's heart was for Lot. We might like to think that he was that well-disposed to the whole city, but this was not necessarily the case. His prayer for Sodom was really a prayer for Lot, his nephew, because he lived there.

Now God in fact did deliver Lot. He did not however do this by saving Sodom from destruction.

God is sovereign in the way he answers our prayers. We cannot demand a particular type of answer. Rather, it is our place to wait humbly and submissively on God for an answer in his terms.

This was the situation in Paul's experience with the thorn in his flesh. God did not remove the thorn. His prayer was persistent, for he prayed three times. We can be in no doubt either that it was earnest. The answer though was 'No!'

It is interesting that he did not, apparently, ask again. He may well have been aware of a parallel with Christ's prayer in Gethsemane, when he asked, three times over, for the cup to be removed from him. Perhaps Paul felt it to be inappropriate to ask more often than the Lord himself had done.

We do not know how God spoke to him, but speak he did. He became aware of a word from God related to the situation. 'But he said to me, "My grace is sufficient for you, for my power is made perfect in weakness" ' (2 Cor. 12:9).

We see again here that grace and power are closely related to each other, although this time in the experience of suffering.

The New Testament shows clearly the influence of Hebrew literary forms. This is because its writers were so steeped in the older inspired literature that their very style was affected by its cadences and assonances.

The chief Hebrew poetic form is known as identical parallelism. This is used over and over again, especially in the psalms and the prophets. In this, the same thought is repeated in different ways. It has the effect of reinforcing what is said. God's double statement to Paul here is a clear example of it.

This means then that in this passage power and grace are virtually synonymous.

Power is what many a sufferer longs to have, not physical power but inner strength, strength to endure what otherwise might be unendurable. If we could be assured that this was available to us, the prospect of suffering would seem a little less fearsome.

This was the assurance Paul was given. He would receive this gracious power and God would himself be its Author. He knew himself to be weak, but he knew too that God was his strength.

To know these two facts and to give them equal weight

is an important key to the spiritual life for every Christian.

He experienced the grace of God in martyrdom

We have no account of Paul's martyrdom, although there is firm evidence for it in early church tradition. We do not know therefore how he actually faced the moment of death.

We do however possess a very late letter from him, his Second Letter to Timothy.

This letter contains these stirring words: 'For I am already being poured out like a drink offering, and the time has come for my departure. I have fought the good fight, I have finished the race, I have kept the faith. Now there is in store for me the crown of righteousness, which the Lord, the righteous Judge, will award to me on that day - and not only to me, but also to all who have longed for his appearing' (2 Tim. 4:6-8).

This shows how he viewed the approach of death. No doubt he was already experiencing a foretaste of that grace which would be his on the day of his martyrdom.

Sometimes a Christian will ask himself how he would fare if called on to face death for the sake of Christ. He may look at his weakness and fear and dread the possibility of failing his Lord when the time came.

What is the answer for such a Christian? Grace! It has been well said that God reserves dying grace for dying moments. That he makes it available is beyond doubt.

For, when all has been said, what is grace? Grace is simply God embracing me with the fullness of his favour, and doing it, not by giving me help at arm's length, but by standing by me. More than that, in fact, by indwelling me by his Spirit.

If that God is for me then, who can be against me?

With confidence in the grace of God he faced the judgement seat of Christ

Paul knew that Christ had borne God's judgement on sin and that there was no longer any threat of condemnation for those who were in Christ. He asserts this very clearly at the start of Romans 8.

Then, as that wonderful chapter moves towards its close, he pens a great series of rhetorical questions. In verse 34, he asks, 'Who is he that condemns? Christ Jesus, who died - more than that, who was raised to life - is at the right hand of God and is also interceding for us.'

In other words, all God has done for us in Christ proclaims our forgiveness, our acceptance, our freedom from condemnation.

Does this mean then that Christians do not have a judgement to face? No, for Paul writes of this very clearly in the very same letter. He says, 'For we will all stand before God's judgment seat ... each of us will give an account of himself to God' (Rom. 14:10-12; cf. 2 Cor. 5:10).

What does this mean? Murray Harris writes helpfully on this when he says:

'Appearance before Christ's tribunal is the privilege of Christians. It is concerned with the assessment of works and, indirectly, of character, not with the determination of destiny; with reward, not status. Judgment on the basis of works is not opposed to justification on the basis of faith ... Yet not all verdicts will be comforting. The believer may "suffer loss" (1 Cor. 3:15) by forfeiting Christ's praise or losing a reward that might have been his.' [1]

So then, as the Christian looks forward to meeting his Lord, it is with great joy and overflowing thankfulness, but also with a realization of the importance of taking disciple-ship seriously. It is those who behave as faithful stewards of God's precious gift of life who will hear him say, 'Well done, good and faithful servant! You have been faithful with a few things; I will put you in charge of many things. Come and share your master's happiness' (Matt. 25:23).

References

1. Murray J. Harris. '2 Corinthians' in F. E. Gaebelein. *Expositor's Bible Commentary*, Vol. 10. Grand Rapids. 1976. on 2 Cor. 5:9,10 *ad loc.*

20

Problems Unlimited In One Church

One of Paul's major roles was that of trouble-shooter.

We have seen him in this role in many of our chapters. What a host of problems he had to deal with in the churches! Theological problems, squabbles between people and parties, unacceptable morality, and many other difficulties.

But some pastor or elder may be feeling our study of Paul has not yet got to grips with the kind of situations that are facing him. You see, the trouble with problems is that they do not always come singly, following each other in orderly sequence, like a series of questions on an examination paper, to be answered one at a time.

So we will now look at one of the Pauline churches and see how Paul dealt with the complex tangle of problems to be found in it.

Which church to choose? Well, it really chooses itself! We have more of Paul's correspondence with the Corinthian church than with any other. Not only so, but his first letter is actually structured by the series of problems he handles. There is plenty of evidence in the second letter too of problems in this church.

We will try to get a fairly comprehensive view of their problems through the two letters to them we possess.

It is not always easy to understand the situation he was addressing in any particular letter. We are not usually in a position to know in any detail what was happening in the churches. Sometimes we feel rather like a person trying to understand one end of a telephone conversation. It is difficult enough in a letter like Galatians, where the whole letter addresses one problem. It is much more difficult in one like Colossians, where the heretics probably had their own distinctive terminology and we cannot always be sure whether Paul was using their own terms against them, and even exactly what those terms meant.

As far as Corinth is concerned, however, we have a big advantage. Paul wrote his first letter on the basis of his knowledge of the problems there. This knowledge came from two sources.

The first of these was a report from some visitors who had given him first-hand information about the church (1 Cor. 1:11). It was they who had told him of the party-spirit and also probably about the ethical problems.

The second source was a letter he had received from them, in which they raised a number of questions. From the beginning of chapter 7 onwards, he addresses these issues one by one.

This means then that he spells out some of the problems quite explicitly, and that is a great help to us as we see how he deals with them.

His two letters to them were both written out of his deep God-given pastoral concern. In fact the pastoral heart of Paul was, humanly speaking, the motivation of all his letters. What he has to say about theology, about ethics, about personal relationships, and so on, all comes in a pastoral context. In this, he was a true disciple of the Good Shepherd.

His readers are people who have responded to the gospel message and have put their trust in the crucified and risen Saviour. So, as we have seen many times in this study, his reference point is the gospel. It is helpful to be able to see how this works out as he approaches the many problems of one church.

Doctrinal error and gospel truth

At the start of 1 Corinthians 15, he reminds them of the nature of the gospel he had declared to them. This gospel was foundational to all good teaching.

It is significant that this comes here. He is just about to deal with a doctrinal error. He wants to make it clear that, logically, this error undermines the good news of Jesus.

Some at Corinth may have wondered what all the fuss was about in this matter of the resurrection of the dead. Why not simply say that the soul survives the death of the body? Surely you could still have an attractive Christian hope along these lines!

No, says Paul; it won't do. Even if you can salvage something for the destiny of the Christian, and that is doubtful in itself, to eliminate the resurrection would mean that death had defeated the Son of God! He is a real man, so the irreversible destruction of every human body must include his. What a devastating conclusion!

The Corinthian Christians may not have thought things through like this. Paul is therefore acting as a faithful pastor in pointing all this out to them and helping them to see it clearly.

He goes back to first principles. He looks at the error, he looks at the gospel, and he judges the former in terms of its faithfulness to the latter. He finds it to be seriously wanting.

We learn something very important here. We learn that the gospel matters enormously.

If we encounter unusual teaching, we must always ask

how it affects the gospel. Does it undermine it or modify it in some way or other? Is the gospel presentation as clear and unambiguous if this teaching is taken on board or is it compromised in some way?

There needs to be good theological teaching in a local church, otherwise that church will be weak and a prey to every doctrinal wind that blows. There are plenty of such winds blowing today, within as well as outside the evangelical churches.

Party-spirit and gospel unity

Party-spirit was a marked feature of church life at Corinth. Paul shows great concern about it.

He traces the root of the problem to wrong attitudes. The Corinthians valued particular qualities they believed certain leaders to possess. Yet these qualities were not necessarily distinctive of the Christian faith.

They valued knowledge, wisdom and power, each of which has a non-Christian as well as a Christian form. No doubt Apollos, for instance, was eloquent even before he became a Christian. There is little indication of concern with the holiness or love of the leaders they chose.

Not only so, but they put them on pedestals. They treated them as if they were very important, and perhaps were in danger of thinking they could do no wrong.

There was danger that the situation might get many times worse. Paul, Apollos and Peter were at least all godly men. No doubt Apollos and Peter would share Paul's distaste for the use of their names by the parties.

There were though new leaders striving to find acceptance, and in many cases finding it. No doubt the same shallow criteria were being applied to them by the church.

In fact, these 'false apostles' (2 Cor. 11:13) were arrogant and appear to have been complete charlatans.

Our true allegiance should be to Christ. We are gospel people.

We are thankful for the human channels through whom the good news of Jesus has come to us, but we should never make too much of them. They may let us down very badly. They may present an image of Christian character that does not fit the gospel they proclaim. This does not invalidate the gospel.

To get taken up with personalities is very dangerous. Think of Jonesville! Think of Waco! Many cult leaders are strong personalities, often very attractive to others. Their attraction has been natural, not spiritual. What matters most in a teacher is his message, with his life illustrating it in terms of character and conduct.

How then did Paul handle the party-spirit at Corinth? He directed attention to the cross of Christ. Here is the wisdom and power so revered by the Corinthians. Here is God's eloquent message which does not need to be conveyed through human eloquence.

It is the seed of this gospel of the cross that matters. Paul and Apollos simply have differing functions in its cultivation. It is Christ who is the Foundation of the church, laid in the preaching of the gospel..

All this comes, of course, in 1 Corinthians 1-4. There is, though, much else in this letter that would minister positively to the situation. In particular, in chapter 12 he uses the analogy of the body to show we all need each other. He makes no reference there to the party-spirit, but the implications for this will not have been lost on them.

It is the gospel that unites Christians. We may have some

differences of emphasis when it comes to matters of practice and even some divergence on secondary theological points, but it is the biblical gospel that unites us.

It is interesting and significant to note that it is in evangelism, more than in anything else, that evangelical churches have found common ground in modern times.

If this is true across local church and even denominational boundaries, it is equally true within a particular local church. Christians there may have different approaches, for instance, to worship styles, but things are seriously wrong if they cannot unite in a deep Spirit-given gospel concern for their neighbourhood and go out to reach its people for Christ.

Lax behaviour and gospel discipline

The God we worship is deeply concerned for the holiness of his people and for their consequent witness in a world that cares little for his standards. The church is the body of Christ on earth and so should reflect his holiness.

Calvin defined a true church as one where the word is preached, the sacraments administered and there is a godly discipline. All three are in fact intimately related to the gospel and so to each other.

This means that some discipline must be maintained in the church. It is not easy to do this.

It must be exercised with great care and with much prayer. There must be constant concern for God's purposes in discipline, for the good of the offender and of others and for the clarity of the church's witness to Christ.

Is discipline in any way related to the gospel? Yes. The preached message calls for repentance and faith. In repentance we turn our backs on our old lives and embrace the will of God in Christ.

Discipline is part of God's plan for deepening that repentance. He shows us our faults that we may seek grace to amend our lives at these points. Discipline is therefore an aspect of the whole Christian life. In the church its administration should always keep pastoral ends in view. Its purpose is to conform church and individual believer to Christ.

So Paul calls the church to exercise this disciplinary function. It is of course very important that this should not be a function of a legalistic outlook, but a truly gracious holiness, in which, in conscious dependence on Christ, we co-operate with his Spirit and seek to do God's will.

If there is conduct which raises serious questions about a person's Christian standing, and the whole community is aware of this, Paul exhorts the church to take excommunicating action.

There must be a clear testimony to the world. This does not imply the perfection of the members, none of whom can afford to adopt a self-righteous attitude. The very fact that we have found salvation in Christ shows our sense of unworthiness. The habitual and public practice of a sinful lifestyle must, however, be taken seriously.

Paul deals with a case of incest in 1 Corinthians 5. He is troubled, not only at the church's apparent lack of concern, but also its haughty attitude (1 Cor. 5:1,2,6). The whole matter was a black mark, not only against the man himself but against the whole local church. Arrogance should be replaced by sorrowful penitence.

The words he uses here, and the procedure they indicate have been much discussed. First of all he says, 'Shouldn't you rather have been filled with grief and have put out of your fellowship the man who did this?' He then goes on to say, 'Even though I am not physically present, I am with you in spirit. And I have already passed judgment on the one who did this, just as if I were present. When you are assembled in the name of our Lord Jesus and I am with you in spirit, and the power of our Lord Jesus is present, hand this man over to Satan, so that the sinful nature may be destroyed and his spirit saved on the day of the Lord' (1 Cor. 5:2-5).

Whatever can this mean?

He sees discipline as an action of God but mediated in this case through the church. It is the church's responsibility to take action. He himself concurs in it, indeed commands it in his apostolic capacity, but it must be their action. When it takes place though it is the disciplining act of God of which the man will become aware.

There is little doubt that Paul is here speaking about excommunication and physical suffering, perhaps by some form of illness. The language is strong and is difficult to tone down. It recognizes a Satanic factor in suffering, for in a world unaffected by evil there would be no suffering at all.

We cannot be sure how long this had been going on and whether Paul would have recommended such severe and dramatic action had it been less long-standing. The fact that it was now a scandal in the community may have determined the nature of the action he exhorts them to take.

Disorderly services and gospel worship

There was no lack of vigour and spontaneity in the Corinthian services. They were so noisy as to be unedifying. Constant chattering, simultaneous prophesying and uninterpreted tongues do not build churches. Whatever would an unbeliever think if he were to come through the doors seeking for the truth?

Then there was the Lord's Supper (1 Cor. 11:17-34). What disgraceful things were happening at it! It was made the occasion of a communal meal, and people were showing discourtesy and sheer greed, when they were supposed to be remembering with thanksgiving the death of Jesus for their sins!

Without doubt such things are not peculiar to Corinth.

Noise itself is not necessarily to be frowned upon. A great congregation singing its full-throated praise to God certainly produces some decibels, but noise is not desirable for its own sake. It is essential that everything be done for the glory of God and also for the edification of the church. What is the value of messages from God if nobody can hear or understand them?

What is gospel worship? We get a picture of what it is ultimately to be in Revelation 4 and 5. Here we see the Lamb of God in the midst of the throne of God and the praises of the redeemed being addressed to him. They praise him because he is worthy of praise. At the centre of their affirmations about him is the fact that he has redeemed them by his blood.

Now this is true of course on earth of the Lord's Supper. In observing this we do not see Christ literally. The bread and wine symbolize his body and blood but they are in no sense actually that body and blood.

He is present spiritually with his people but their worship is directed to him because he gave himself for them at infinite personal cost. It is because of this that there is to be no disorderly behaviour, no participation in an unworthy manner. In other words, we must never forget the nature of the supper and its central significance as a thankful calling to mind of Christ's death for us.

There is a picture too of worship in 1 Corinthians,

chapters 12 to 14. This worship affirms Christ's Lordship (12:1ff), which is for ever established by his resurrection from the dead.

The church is Christ's body and the activity of the Holy Spirit in its life, which includes its worship, is to be expressed through its members. So we all have a part to play in worship. Worship can never be simply the activity of one person.

So true gospel order in worship will not stifle but give orderly expression to the worship of its members, and that worship will be directed to the crucified and risen Christ, and to the Father through him.

Dilatory giving and gospel generosity

Paul gave the Corinthians directions about the collection for the poor Christians at Jerusalem (1 Cor. 16). He advised regularity in putting aside the money to be used for this purpose.

When he wrote his second letter, however, there is a gentle note of censure.

He does not doubt their generosity. They have in fact already proved this, for they had shown great eagerness to give and had in fact given handsomely a year ago.

Now however another gift is needed, and they have been somewhat dilatory in getting money together for this purpose. His whole desire is to spur them on.

Sometimes financial decisions in a church may take some time to carry into effect. If money has been set aside for some specific project in the Lord's work, is there any reason why it should not be sent straight away? If there is no compelling reason for delay, why should not those in need have it right now?

Of course, a church may be not only dilatory but niggardly and this is more serious still. With all its faults, there is no evidence of this in the church at Corinth. What is it that motivates Christian giving? Paul handles this question in 2 Corinthians 8 and 9.

Is it human need? Of course this plays a part. Undoubtedly Paul's own heart was touched by the plight of the poor Christian believers in Jerusalem. Our own hearts today would be stony if the crying need of people for physical and most of all for spiritual help did not touch them.

This cannot however be the basis of Christian giving. Like a call to a specific field of service, it must be grounded in God, not in man.

To what then does Paul appeal? He writes of the generosity of God in Christ. He extols the humble self-giving of Christ who for our sakes became poor that we might be rich through him. Clearly he was not thinking simply of the poverty of the Galilean Preacher but of the deep, deep poverty of Calvary. It is not simply through the life of Christ but through his death that we are made rich.

So, it is out of thankfulness for the gospel, gratitude to Jesus himself, that we want to give to those whose need is great. Is the poverty of our giving perhaps testimony to the fact that Christ's great sacrifice on our behalf does not occupy our minds as much as it should?

Incomplete conversion and gospel holiness

Most of these folk had been converted from a background of deeply immoral paganism. When we consider their background, we are not surprised at some of the problems Paul faced in the church there.

They would have been used to an attitude to religion in

which unworthy beings were accorded worship, in which sacred prostitution played a part and in which there was no moral content at all.

They were used to a society where gross paganism existed side by side with a sophisticated philosophical interest, with its accompanying intellectual snobbery, and where fine rhetoric and high-sounding language were highly valued. Some of the philosophers may have held aloof from the worst excesses of the worship, but were unlikely to have condemned it strongly.

If there were low moral standards in the church, these were undoubtedly due to the influence of the environment. It was not simply a question of being still exposed to temptation from it, but also of the influence it exerted on them unconsciously.

This happens of course in every day and generation and in every type of society. Without doubt it happens in the church in the West today. Do Christians ever cheat the tax man? Do Christians ever show antagonism to each other, or act arrogantly towards each other? Do Christian marriages ever break up because of unfaithfulness? We all know the answer to these questions.

In fact, it has to be admitted that our own society is becoming more and more like that at Corinth all the time. How good it is that we have Paul's letters to that church for our lasting benefit!

Holiness in the Bible has to do with separation, with distinctness. Through his death and resurrection, Christ has sanctified us. He has set us apart for God who himself is the holy, the distinct, One.

Because we have been set apart in this way, we are then to be holy. We are to be what we are. In other words, we are to live in a way that is consistent with what God has done for us already in Christ.

Now, for the Corinthian Christians, this meant separation from the lifestyle of their environment. Like the Thessalonians (1 Thess. 1:9,10), they had turned to God from idols to serve the living and true God. Now the implications of this separation to the true God which was at the same time a separation from paganism needed to be seen and acted upon.

This means there could be no question of participating in pagan worship. They could not sit at the table of demons and also sit at the table of Christ. Such would be unthinkable.

This is something we all have to learn. The cross of Christ judges our values.

We may not be guilty of literal idolatry, although if a Christian should take his horoscope seriously he is getting close to literal paganism. We can however make something too much the centre of our lives. We may be worshippers of Christ on Sundays and yet worshippers of money from Monday to Friday and of sport on Saturday.

This is not to say that money and sport can have no place in the Christian life, but it does mean they should never be the centre, not simply on the Lord's day but on any day.

So many problems!

This study of the Corinthian church has certainly shown us that its problems were many-sided. In this way it is like many a modern church.

It is encouraging though to find that Paul was still thankful for the church and also that he did not abandon it, because, of course, he knew that Christ had not abandoned it.

He would perhaps have appreciated the modern Christian poster which reads, 'Be patient with me; God has not finished with me yet.' How thankful we can be that this is true both of imperfect Christians and of imperfect churches!

Not only so, but he never took his eyes off Christ. It is the Christ who showed such amazing patience with twelve very imperfect men during his earthly ministry who is the Lord of the church.

That same Christ is able to give patience to those of us who serve him and at the same time to remind us of his patience with us too!

21

Paul and the Modern Church

At the beginning of our study, we asked the question, 'Why Paul?' I wonder if the book has answered that question more fully than the first chapter did? Hopefully it has.

It may be though that you still feel you need some help in applying what Paul did and said to the situation of the churches today. We have tried to give some indications of the contemporary relevance of this study on our way through, but it would perhaps be useful to set out here some clear principles to guide us.

In this chapter, we will start with the modern church and its problems. We will then look at Paul's life and writings to see how far these help us with our problems.

Inevitably some generalization is unavoidable. After all, what is this 'modern church' we are talking about? Is it Episcopal, Presbyterian or Independent? Is it Charismatic or Reformed? Is it large or small? Is it western or eastern, predominantly middle-class or working-class, racially mixed or unmixed?

'The modern church' is an abstraction, as 'the average man' is. Just as there is nobody in the whole world who actually has 2.4 children (we can certainly be glad of that!), so this 'modern church', this finely-balanced, statistically-averaged monstrosity, does not exist.

No, but yours does and so does mine! No doubt your church and mine differ a good deal, but of this we can be sure: there will be blessings and problems in them both.

Unfortunately, a Christian may sometimes find himself deeply dissatisfied with the church to which he belongs. Of course, this sometimes tells the observer more about the Christian than about the church, but there is no doubt that this dissatisfaction may be justified.

This may be true for you. At the very least, however, the Scriptures will be read publicly and there is always blessing in that when our ears are open to hear what God has to say to us. If the Bible is never opened it is certainly time you went somewhere else!

We will look at six of the main areas in which problems may arise in a church at the present day.

These are not exhaustive as you will quickly see.

For instance, churches in many lands have had problems in dealing with their relationship to the State, and we do not touch on that here. Inevitably our preoccupation is somewhat with the British situation, although the six problem areas are common to churches in many lands.

Theological confusion
This is very widespread.

At one time, say in the first half of the 19th century, the doctrinal lines were drawn very clearly in most of the churches.

If you were a Presbyterian you went to the Westminster Confession or the Shorter Catechism for your doctrine, if you were an Anglican it was the Thirty-Nine Articles. Churches which did not have such explicitly detailed doctrinal standards nevertheless taught the main outlines of their belief clearly. Even churches like those of the Christian Brethren, who emphasized that the Bible alone was their standard of doctrine, tended to be in broad agreement with each other on theological matters.

Even a fairly superficial acquaintance with the contemporary church scene makes the observer aware of the fact that the situation is very different today. What are the main factors that have brought about the change?

First of all, there was the advent of theological liberalism, with its increasing influence on the churches. Liberalism is not easy to define, but it involves the profession of Christian faith combined with reductionist views on the authority of Scripture. When the authority of the Bible was being undermined, of course, other aspects of the church's doctrine could not remain unaffected, because Scripture is the source of this doctrine.

Liberalism passed through a number of stages, each phase being dominated by a different philosophical outlook. Of course, churchmen with this point of view are still very much with us. Their names get into the newspapers, and they appear on television.

Then there was the coming of the ecumenical movement. During the 19th century, the denominational lines began to become a little less rigid. Christians began to co-operate with each other, first of all on Bible translation and publishing, then in evangelism and missionary work. The great host of para-church organisations, as they are called, is due very largely to this co-operation.

In the 20th Century however there has been an increasingly strong promotion of the idea of organic union between churches and groups of churches. At first, this simply involved churches which were fairly close doctrinally already, sharing perhaps a Presbyterian organisation or a Methodist theology of the Christian life. More recently, however, there has been a concern to unite churches which vary much more widely in their outlook.

What has affected theology has been the tendency, often accompanying this, to play down the importance of doctrine. It is said that doctrine is a divisive factor.

Then, around 1960, the Charismatic Movement came into existence. This was of course preceded by Pentecostalism. The Pentecostals had established new church groups, but many charismatics remained in their own denominations. Apart from the doctrine of the Spirit, many charismatics too have tended to play down the importance of theology or even to regard it as merely cerebral and so of little value for true Christian growth. There are of course outstanding exceptions.

What has characterized all three movements has been their widespread influence across denominational boundaries. Also there have often been considerable differences of outlook even within local churches.

What would Paul have done in such a situation? Probably two things.

He would have given good, balanced, biblical teaching. In the teaching he gave to the churches of his day he brought out from the gospel its theological, ethical and social implications. No doubt he would do this today, making specific application to our particular problems. So we need to know what the Scriptures teach, and to see that good theological understanding becomes the heritage of all who become members of Christ's church in our day.

Then Paul would have given special attention to theological issues on which there was confusion. In 1 Corinthians 12-15, he did this quite explicitly. He dealt with issues in as much detail as was necessary to deal with the situation. The

first three of these four chapters are very helpful to us, for
they deal with the use of spiritual gifts, a very lively issue
today.

The point we wish to stress is the importance of frank
and open teaching. Theological thistles need to be grasped.
At a time of theological confusion Christians need help, and
only clear teaching and open discussion of difficulties will
be of any real value to them.

Differences over worship

I preach in a good many churches. These churches belong
to quite a number of denominations and to none. Wherever
I go, there is one subject which is constantly being discussed, and that is worship. It is undoubtedly the major
talking point in the churches today.

There is the battle of the hymn books, the Psalter, the
song books, the overhead projector. Which should we use?
It is not a matter of Ancient and Modern, but rather of
ancient or modern?

There is the battle of the versions. Which should we read
from the pulpit? AV? RSV? NEB? NIV? GNB? NKJB?
What a plethora of initials!

There is the battle of the instruments. Should it be the
organ, the piano, the band, the synthesizer, or perhaps just
the tuning fork?

There is the battle of worship leadership. Should it be the
young musician, the older elder or deacon, or the middle-
aged minister?

There is the battle of the physical actions. To stand, to sit,
to kneel, to raise hands, to clap hands, to dance? Which
should we do?

Apart from these issues, although intertwined with some

of them, is the many-sided battle of the spiritual gifts, and how, if at all, they are to be exercised in our church services.

What guidance can we get from Paul, or rather from the Lord of the church through him?

In Ephesians 5:18-20 and Colossians 3:15-17, Paul writes about the church's worship. What can we learn when we take these two passages together?

We see that in worship we are to be at one with each other as Christ's body. There is to be an atmosphere of deep gratitude, and therefore of joy. There is to be instruction and the songs employed in worship are to have good teaching content. Then the people are to go out from worship to serve God in the same spirit of thankfulness.

All this is to be an expression of the fullness of the Spirit and of the controlling influence of the word of Christ, the gospel. In the Ephesians passage Paul says, 'be filled with the Spirit!' while in Colossians it is, 'Let the word of Christ dwell in you richly!'

These are not really two facts, but two sides of the same fact. Fullness and rich indwelling are different ways of indicating control. To be controlled in every part of the service by the gospel of Christ, and by the word of God interpreted in terms of it, is to have a congregation filled with the Spirit. Obedient response to Christ and to the Holy Spirit must be one fact, not two.

In 1 Corinthians 12 to 14, we see something of the variety of forms in which the word came to encourage and strengthen the church. In these chapters, one of Paul's leading concerns is with order. He is not thinking of an order which stifles the Spirit but rather of one in which his activity may find full expression.

The Holy Spirit was active in the creation of the universe,

in the bringing of order out of formlessness. He will not work in order in the old creation and in disorder in the new.

Unless there is order the church cannot be edified, and unless the church is edified, God is not glorified. This was true in Paul's day; it is no less true today.

Vibrant spiritual life and firm and helpful order - these should never be separated. We may not get an answer to all our questions about worship, but this will help us with some of the more important of them.

The Moral Influence of Society

It is a commonplace of Christian comment on society today that moral standards have fallen greatly in recent decades and that they are continuing to slide.

It is usual to point particularly to the area of sexual morality, and the constant deterioration here cannot be denied. We should not however concentrate exclusively on this. Violence has enormously increased, but so also has general dishonesty.

Do not forget though that evil has also affected the very structures of our society. There have been too many questions about the integrity of the police and there is much public dissatisfaction with the kind of sentences often handed down in the courts.

There has also been legislation on abortion, on genetic engineering and in several other areas, that has deeply upset many Christians.

But what about the church? We cannot pretend that the tendencies we observe in the world around us have left our churches untouched. This is anything but true.

Can we find in Paul's life and letters any guidance for our modern situation? Most certainly we can.

The apostle took seriously the sexual misdemeanours of various sorts which were evident in his society. These were endemic at Corinth and they are now endemic in ours. In Romans 1 he wrote very strongly about homosexual conduct. In 1 Corinthians 5 we see that he considered incest an abomination to God. His epistles contain strong exhortations against fornication and adultery.

A course of sermons from time to time on the Ten Commandments and their application to modern life would do none of our modern churches any harm!

Is the level of follow-up instruction given in connection with evangelistic crusades adequate on the ethical side? We cannot of course generalize, but in many cases it appears quite inadequate.

Perhaps the hesitation to give such instruction is due to a fear of introducing legalism into the outlook of people who have just entered a wonderful experience of God's grace in Christ. There certainly could be a danger of this. If however ethical teaching is shown to emerge from the gospel itself, there need be no fear of this.

The churches of New Testament times appear to have taught their people the basics of Christian ethics, especially in connection with social relationships. Surely then we need to teach new converts Christian ethical standards!

Financial administration

How should churches that profess to be biblical be organized?

This is a highly contentious question. There has been debate for centuries between those who favour differing forms of church government. We are certainly not going to debate episcopacy, presbyterianism and congregationalism here! There are nevertheless issues of church administration that we can helpfully discuss within the pages of this book. We will look at just one of them - how the money of a local church should be handled.

We cannot deny that there have been instances of financial maladministration in modern churches. These have sometimes been investigated by the media, and everything has been exposed to public view. It is needless to say that this does great harm to the testimony of a local church.

Paul was very scrupulous in his handling of the money subscribed by the Gentile churches for the benefit of the poor Christians in Jerusalem. There was no question even of a man of his integrity travelling alone with the money. Representatives of the churches went with him (2 Cor. 8:16-21). He knew how important the public testimony of the church was in such matters. The Graeco-Roman world was full of charlatans, and religious charlatans at that, and Christianity had to be shown to be different.

The lessons for us are clear. Everything in church finance must be public and above board. Enquiries from church members should be dealt with frankly and openly. It is true that a treasurer has to preserve a measure of confidentiality in relation to some matters, but structures need to be devised that will secure financial security and accountability.

Personality problems

We all find some people more attractive than others. 'Why it is, I cannot tell, I do not like thee, Doctor Fell.'

Some modern churches have been split apart and some utterly destroyed as a result of conflict between members and especially between leaders.

It is true that sometimes the result has been the planting

of a church in another area, with a further centre of gospel witness to the community. How much better though for this to come about as a result of guidance given to the whole church without strife or discord. It is not a good start to the witness of a new church if the people who live near get to know that its very existence is due to acrimony resulting in a split.

Now, as we have seen, Paul and Barnabas fell out on one occasion. We have no means of ascertaining clearly the rights and wrongs of that situation. Certainly it did mean that the two men led teams to two areas.

The issue in the clash with Peter is clear. Peter probably did not realise this, but the gospel itself was at stake in the issue.

Where this is the case, Christians must take a stand. There can be no compromise on this. It must be done courteously, and, if at all possible, quietly, but it must be done. No concern for tolerance nor desire for peace should be allowed to compromise the gospel itself. The letter to the Galatians is sufficient witness to this.

But it has to be admitted that many of the issues over which Christians fall out are extremely trivial.

What mattered at Philippi was not that Syntyche should give up her point of view and accept the outlook of Euodia, nor vice versa. Paul simply says to them that they should be of the same mind in the Lord. The disharmony between them was in fact much more important than the issue itself. It was Christian grace that was needed, a diffusion of the love of Christ that would bring a new love between these two women.

It is surprising that we do not read more about personality clashes in the story of Paul's life and in the letters that came from his pen. Perhaps this is because the Spirit of God was so evidently at work in the Pauline churches. It is a complete openness of our churches to the authority of God, to the word of Christ, to the fullness of the Holy Spirit (three ways of saying the same thing) and not leadership manipulation that is going to deal with problems like that.

Evangelistic Outreach

The Corinthians wrote Paul a letter in which they asked his advice on a number of matters. It is interesting and instructive to consider not only the issues they raised with him but also those they did not.

There is one that might well have featured prominently in a letter from them to Paul, and yet apparently it did not. What is that? It is the issue of effective evangelistic outreach.

They lived in a large city in which they saw every day how much the people needed Christ. Why did they not write to Paul asking him to give them some guidance about how to reach their city and its people with the good news of Jesus? Did they feel a great burden as they walked its streets, as they saw the way its people were devoting their lives to money, to illicit sex, to religious objects that were totally unworthy, and mistaking the eloquence of the clever orator for truth?

Were they grieved as they saw their city wholly given to idolatry? If so, their appeal would undoubtedly have found its mark in the heart of Paul, for that was exactly how he had felt in Athens. It was not the beauty of the buildings on the Acropolis which he saw, but their dedication to false gods. The Venus de Milo is greatly admired for its sculptured beauty, but we should remember that this was the same goddess as the notorious Aphrodite worshipped at Corinth.

What then are we to make of this silence on the part of the Corinthian Christians?

They may, of course, have been so well taught in this regard by Paul or others that they did not need advice. On the other hand, they may have been so preoccupied with the internal problems of their church that they had become inward-looking.

There is perhaps just a hint of this in Paul's comment about uninterpreted tongues (1 Cor. 14:22-25). He was concerned about the unbeliever who might come in and find himself totally at a loss to understand what was going on. Such an unbeliever might conclude that the Christians were mad. In addition, of course, he might not hear the gospel of Christ at all in a language he could understand. It looks as if the Corinthians had not considered this sort of thing.

Then there was the Lord's Supper. This too was disorderly. Paul reminded them that through this Supper a proclamation of Christ is made (1 Cor. 11:26). This too is a glance at the outsider who might come into the service.

Also, he was concerned about the testimony of the church to those outside. This was why he was so appalled by the fact that they went to law before unbelievers (1 Cor. 6: 1,6). He himself was willing to become all things to all men that he might by all possible means save some (1 Cor. 9:22). All he did was done for the sake of the gospel.

So it is Paul's attitude, not the outlook of the Corinthian church, or indeed of any other New Testament church, that ought to be a spur to us.

Do we have the same great concern for the gospel as he had? Are we prepared for sacrifices, and do we consider the affect of conduct within the church on those who come in from the outside? The major test of all our activities in the church must be whether or not these activities glorify God by advancing the cause of the gospel.

Many of our activities are for the benefit of believers. There is no doubt that Christians need to be instructed, challenged, encouraged and comforted. Churches have a responsibility under God to their members.

It is easy however for our local churches to become inward-looking, ghettoes of isolation from the world. It will help to guard them against this kind of outlook if we are constantly asking what gospel relevance our activities have.

This relevance may be indirect. The church members may meet together for social activities. Alright, these may be opportunities for inviting unbelievers so that they may find out that Christians, although different, are not as odd as they thought they were!

Meetings for Christian teaching should in fact prepare the members of the church to be better Christians, and therefore better witnesses in a needy world.

The gospel always has to be kept in mind. It is to make known the good news of Jesus that the church has been left in the world by its Lord.

22

Christ the Answer

All the way through this book, we have been stressing the importance of the gospel for Paul.

Certainly he was guided by the Spirit of God, whose work of inspiration was the factor which gave authority to his teaching. The Spirit often uses means, however, and the message of the gospel seems to have been the objective guiding light which the Holy Spirit used as Paul faced problem after problem.

Now when we say 'the gospel,' what exactly do we mean?

This is a very important question. It is often said that churches which have slightly different points of view on matters of doctrine and practice may find common ground in the gospel and in co-operating in its proclamation.

If this is true, and the present writer certainly believes it is, nothing can be more important than identifying what the gospel actually is. In fact, to go wrong here is to go wrong everywhere. Misunderstand or misrepresent the gospel and the consequences are dire, both for yourself and for those who may be influenced by you.

Is it simply the message that human beings may have a dynamic spiritual experience which will result in a complete reorientation of their lives?

No, true as this is, it is certainly not enough if we say no more than this.

Members of cults that are anything but truly Christian have had such experiences. Devotees of the New Age tell of moments when everything in life began to look and feel different. To begin with an inner experience and come to an understanding of the gospel by this route is fraught with problems. Satan is a master of the subjective counterfeit.

When we say the gospel was Paul's guiding light, do we mean then that he had some specially important formula with which he tested everything?

No, for Paul the gospel was no mere formula. The gospel is in fact Jesus. It is Jesus crucified and risen, but definitely Jesus.

Without him there is no gospel. Show somebody an empty cross and an empty tomb and he could well say, 'So what?' It is the Person who died on the cross and who rose out of that tomb who is vitally important. The gospel is Jesus.

Mind you, the cross and the resurrection are vitally important too.

It must have been wonderful to meet Jesus during the days of his flesh, but people were not saved simply by contact with that wonderful Life. We are sinners, and unless somebody has died for us we will have to carry those sins, and their awful penalty, into eternity. Thank God, Somebody has died for us, and not just anybody, but the one Person who could really deal with those sins. Then, on the third day, he rose in glorious triumph out of that grave.

So, when we say that the gospel is the answer to all the problems and difficulties Paul faced, what we really mean is that Christ, in the gospel, is the Answer.

We need to remember too that the Christ who is the gospel came as the climax of the whole series of Divine acts recorded for us in the Old Testament. Jesus Christ was no isolated phenomenon. He was both the Incarnation and the Action of the great Creator/Redeemer God of the Old Testament. The gospel does not replace the Old Testament; it interprets it.

It is also important to stress that the Christ who is the gospel is the Christ of the New Testament. If 'Christ' is a word with vital meaning, the meaning we must give it is the meaning the New Testament gives it. A conception of Christ that is not true to the New Testament is a Christ of our own making, not the Christ of the gospel.

So, when we say that the gospel was Paul's guiding light in facing his problems, we are not setting the gospel over against the Bible, or implying that there is any kind of gospel-centredness that is not at the same time Bible-centredness.

If however the Bible is to be our guide, we need to ask what is its interpretative centre, the great theme which integrates all its teaching and provides focus for that teaching? This is in fact the gospel.

Bible-centred, gospel-centred, Christ-centred - if we are guided by God's Spirit these will be one for us, for the Bible has the gospel at its heart, and the gospel centres in Christ.

If Christ was God's own Answer to all the problems Paul faced, how will this work out for us, if we, like Paul, are Christ's people by grace through faith.

He is the Answer, for Paul and for us, because:

Christ is our Saviour
Our greatest need is for God's forgiveness.

Through Christ, God has dealt with our sins. No longer

are we under his judgement, no longer are we far from him. But because of Christ's death for us we have been brought near. The great gulf caused by sin has been bridged, from God's side, by his gift of Jesus as our Saviour.

There are all sorts of ways in which this can be expressed, and Paul uses several of these.

Christ is our righteousness (1 Cor. 1:30). How can this be? Because he has taken our sins upon himself, and his righteousness becomes ours by a wonderful gift of God's grace. This means then that, just as Christ is fully accepted in the presence of God, so, by faith in him, are we!

The barrier of sin has gone, the law of God has been vindicated, our guilt has been taken by Somebody else who has made himself fully responsible for it.

This means then that there is no need for us to try and make ourselves right with God by our own efforts. God has done the work himself in Christ, and we can rejoice in this.

Also, Paul writes about the family of God.

Through Christ, we have been brought into that family and we are now the sons and daughters of the living God (Gal. 3:26; 2 Cor. 6: 17,18). Christ is the Son of God by nature, but we are members of the same family by grace. Christ sealed the adoption document with his own blood (Eph. 1:5-7).

If we are righteous through Christ and are members of the family of God, will this make us complacent? If we no longer have to work to achieve our standing before God's law, or to secure entry to his family on merit, does this mean we can simply do as we like?

In fact, both righteousness and sonship are challenging ideas. If Christ's righteousness is made ours, then we ought to seek to live righteous lives.

We cannot do this by ourselves, but we have the Holy Spirit, the Spirit of the perfectly holy One, living within us to enable us to live for him. The challenge to righteous living comes to us time and time again in Paul's letters, and, through the Spirit, there is Divine power available to enable us to make positive response to this.

If we are sons and daughters of God, then people have a right to expect we will show some family likeness. Looking at our characters, they should be able to remark, 'Like Father, like son.' If this is the expectation of our friends, how much more will it be God's own expectation!

So this means that low moral standards should have no place in our thinking. Out of gratitude to our Saviour and through the indwelling power of the Spirit, who is not called the Holy Spirit for nothing, we should be living lives that commend the One we love.

Christ our Life

This finds confirmation when we go on to think about Christ as our Life.

Albert Schweitzer, Adolf Deissmann, James S. Stewart[1] and others have emphasized the importance of union with Christ in Paul's outlook and experience. There can be no doubt about this. The phrase 'in Christ' is as characteristic of his writings as 'through Christ'.

These days interest in mystical spirituality is on the increase. This is not always within a Christian context. There is much interest in various forms of oriental mysticism. New Age spirituality, for instance, has a strong element of this in it.

It is so easy for us to be deceived. This is especially true when heresy speaks the language of orthodoxy, as it so often does. We need to be able to penetrate beyond the mere use of the right words to find out what is being conveyed by them. When a motor-car firm began to advertise a 'born-again car,' this comparatively innocuous use of a biblical expression should have shown Christians that their language could be taken over for purposes far removed from the gospel.

It is important therefore for us to be clear as to what union with Christ meant for Paul. Here was no vague spirituality, no mere heightened consciousness of God, no bypassing of the usual channels of Divine revelation to obtain some direct, unmediated experience of God. The reference to Christ roots this kind of spirituality in history and therefore in facts.

The basis of union with Christ in God's revelation in history is clear.

In writing to the Corinthians, Paul says, 'For if someone comes to you and preaches a Jesus other than the Jesus we preached, or if you receive a different spirit from the one you received, or a different gospel from the one you accepted, you put up with it easily enough!' (2 Cor. 11:4). This is, of course, a rebuke.

There is no place for 'another Jesus'. We cannot construct our own picture of Jesus, even by selecting some characteristics of the historical Jesus and ignoring others. A Jesus who is human but not divine, who is a prophet but not a priest, who teaches us but does not die for us, who talked about love but never about judgement, this is not the Jesus of the New Testament nor of the letters of Paul. He would certainly have identified such a 'Jesus' as belonging to 'another gospel'.

The Jesus Christ with whom he was united was the Jesus

Christ of the Gospels, but now risen and exalted. Here then is no mere mystical experience which can be invested with any number of optional qualities, taking its colour from the desires and background of the person who has it.

The link between union with Christ and the central Christian facts is also clear. Paul brings this out in powerful fashion in Romans 6 when he writes of union with Christ in his death and resurrection.

Here is no soft option, an alternative to that humble dependence on a crucified Saviour which is the proper response to the gospel. There is no dichotomy between Romans 3 and Romans 6. The Christ who is our Redeemer and our justifying Substitute is also the One to whom we are united. Union with Christ is itself a fruit of Christ's redemptive work, and the means by which we receive the benefits of that work.

Moreover there is no loss of identity in this union.

It is true that Paul says that 'he who unites himself with the Lord is one with him in spirit' (1 Cor. 6:17). What does this mean?

He certainly does not mean by this that the believer is merged in Christ, lost in him as the drop of rain water is in the sea. Always Christ is Lord and we are his servants. We may be members of his body, vitally united to him by the Holy Spirit, but we are still responsible and must all appear before God's judgement seat (Rom. 14:10).

Nevertheless many Christians have not taken this great doctrine of union with Christ as fully into their thinking about the Christian faith and life as they might have done.

Here is great encouragement, for if we are joined to him, his life flows in us through the Spirit. We should therefore set no arbitrary limits to what God can do in us,

Here too is great challenge. If the Christ to whom we are united is a Christ so wedded to the will of God that he went to the cross, then his life in us should take the shape of the cross too, in willingness for God's will no matter what the cost.

Here then is a further spur to holiness. Not only are we grateful to him as our Saviour but we are also united to him as our Life.

Christ our Head

The analogy of the body was an important one for Paul. When he develops it in 1 Corinthians 12, you will see that he does not give any special significance to the head. This special significance is spelled out, however, in his later epistles (Eph. 1:22,23; 5:23; Col. 1:18; 2:19).

What was it, for Paul, that united Christians to each other and that made it so important for them to live at peace with each other and to express their unity in many other ways? It is the fact that they are all members of the one body, of which Christ is the Head.

His headship of the body has two important implications.

First of all, it means that it is his life that flows through it and therefore through each member. So, at this level, it is simply a vivid expression for union with Christ.

There is, however, an important second implication. Because Christ is the head of the body, he is the Lord of the church. It is the head that controls the body, so that headship implies government; it signifies authority and control.

So, in the church, there can be no question of the members simply doing their own thing. There is an order there, and this order, when biblically conceived and ex-

pressed, is the result of Christ's headship of the church and
the Holy Spirit's application of that headship in a practical
way.

If we were all to appreciate this, a great many of the
problems in our churches would disappear overnight.

Christ our Lord

Paul's awareness of the Lordship of Christ is profound and
far-reaching. He uses the Greek word *kurios*, Lord, with
great frequency and in the majority of cases in clear
application to Christ.

Now this term was of great significance for Greek-
speaking Jews. When the Septuagint (the main Greek
translation of the Old Testament) was produced, it was used
to translate the great name of God. Paul uses the term with
no reduced meaning.

The New Testament writers employ two great terms in
particular to designate Christ in terms of his deity. There is
'Son of God,' which of course shows his relationship to the
Father to be divine. Then there is 'Lord' which shows his
relationship to us to be divine.

Paul uses the term 'Son of God,' quite sparingly, only
seventeen times altogether, although it has been noticed
that, when he does so, there is a certain elevation of style
associated with his use of it, as if it was a term inducing him
to worship. For instance, he uses it twice in the great closing
section (verses 28 to 39) of Romans 8.

His much greater use of the term 'Lord' indicates, of
course, his preoccupation with the relationship of Jesus to
his people. Paul was concerned with local churches, and the
term 'Lord' was just what was needed to bring out the
importance of Jesus for them. If he was indeed their Lord,

this fact was full of blessing and challenge for them.

Because he is Lord, his church gives him worship. His people do not however worship him as a distant, far-away deity, but as the Lord in the midst of his people.

This means that all worship must reflect what he is and so must be worthy of him. It is under his Lordship too that the Spirit is at work in the churches, imparting spiritual gifts for use in that worship.

It is because he is Lord that humility is essential in those who represent him in the churches. There can be no room for arrogance or elitism, no place for party-spirit, no empire-building by people responsible for particular aspects of the church's life.

So the whole church needs to recognise the Lordship of Jesus and to do so in a thoroughly practical fashion. As the Lord Jesus himself said, 'Why do you call me, "Lord, Lord," and do not do what I say?' (Luke 6:46).

Because he is Lord, his supremacy extends to the whole universe and so, of course, to all human life. Therefore the church, as it goes out to bring the gospel to others, does so in order that his rightful inheritance in the life of every human being may be claimed for him by his people.

Paul's concentration on the gospel, then, was the way in which he stressed the claim of Christ to rule the hearts and lives of men and women everywhere.

It is therefore appropriate for us to ask ourselves, in the presence of God, whether our outlook is controlled by the gospel in the way Paul's was and whether our lives are surrendered in whole-hearted submission to the Christ of the gospel, the Christ of Calvary and of the empty tomb?

Christ is our Hope

People have always asked questions about the future.

These questions are sometimes very general. What is going to happen to the world? Can the human race survive nuclear warfare? global warming? pollution? AIDS?

Sometimes they are very personal. What will happen to me after I die?

Such questions were being asked in Paul's day too, although not in quite the same terms. Paul had no doubt at all about the answer: the future belongs to Christ and therefore to those who are Christ's.

He knew about pollution. Not the physical pollution which bothers us today, but the moral pollution that has been in the world ever since the Fall of the human race into sin.

He knew too that God has taken mankind's defection from him so seriously that he has ordained it should affect the very fabric of the universe (Rom. 8:20). Of course the thorns and thistles and childbirth pains of Genesis 3 are some of the evidence of this.

This is not however to be the final state of things. In Romans 8, Paul goes on to affirm that this bondage to decay will one day end and the universe will know 'the glorious freedom of the children of God'. Why 'of the children of God'? Because all the frustrations, the limitations, the trials and the imperfections of this life will end for God's children when Christ comes again and their very bodies share his glorious likeness (Rom. 8:20-25; cf. 1 Cor. 15:19-58; Phil. 3:20,21; Col. 3:4; 2 Thess. 1:10). What a wonderful hope that is!

Paul looked forward to that day with great eagerness. In the last letter we have from him, he says, 'I have fought the good fight, I have finished the race, I have kept the faith. Now there is in store for me the crown of righteousness, which the Lord, the righteous Judge, will award to me on that day - and not only to me, but also to all who have longed for his appearing' (2 Tim. 4:7-8).

As in Paul's day, churches face problems today, sometimes from external but all too often from internal causes. Individual Christians too, such as you and I, will continue to face difficulties.

Remember though that the future of the church, despite all her problems, is in Christ's hands and that this is true for your life and mine too.

In the resources Christ gives and in the assurance that the future belongs to Christ, Paul was able to face life and to wrestle with the big issues head on.

So can we.

References

1. J.S.Stewart. *A Man in Christ: the vital element in Paul's religion.* London. 1936

SELECT BIBLIOGRAPHY

W. Barclay. *The Mind of St Paul* London and Glasgow. 1965

E. Best. *Paul and his Converts*. Edinburgh. 1988

F.F. Bruce. *Paul: Apostle of the Heart Set Free*. Exeter. 1977

A.M. Hunter. *Paul and his Predecessors*. New Revised Edn. London. 1961

S. Kim. *The Origin of Paul's Gospel*. Tübingen. 1981

J.G. Machen. *The Origin of Paul's Religion*. London. 1921.

A. Murray, *An Apostle's Inner Life*. London. 1989

H.N. Ridderbos. *Paul: An Outline of his Theology*. Grand Rapids. 1975

S. Westerholm, *Israel's Law and the Church's Faith: Paul and His Recent Interpreters*. Grand Rapids. 1988

JA Zeisler. *Pauline Christianity*. Oxford and New York. 1983